BOOK ONE
LITURGICAL YEARS ABC

for use with the Revised
Common Lectionary & the
Book of Common Prayer

D1478056

The Portland Psalter

81 Responsorial Psalms
for congregation, cantor & choir

settings composed
by Robert A. Hawthorne

 CHURCH

Church Publishing, New York

Church Publishing Incorporated
445 Fifth Avenue
New York, NY 10016

5 4 3 2 1

Table of Contents

Alphabetical Psalm Refrain Texts

Refrain texts are abbreviated only for space considerations.

Foreword

I fell in love with the Book of Psalms early in my life. Full of joy and praise, hope and expectation, rage and calls for vengeance, sorrow and despondency, the Psalms speak to me. They affirm my heart, give voice to my spirit and release to my soul. Until I encountered the Episcopal Church as a young adult, my experience with Psalmody was strictly as spoken word or anthem text. What a glorious moment it was to hear the Psalms expressed so wondrously: Anglican chant and plainsong sung by choirs, and responsorial Psalms sung by cantor and congregation.

When I became the Minister of Music at Christ Church in Lake Oswego, Oregon, the Psalms were spoken in the liturgy. It became my mission to bring Psalm singing back to the congregation. At first, I composed responsorial settings as a means to introduce Psalm singing to the people. However, their response was overwhelming. What struck me most was how often I heard the comment, "I found myself singing last Sunday's refrain all week long." The music served the text. And that was the point! So began my odyssey to compose a complete Psalter.

Composing these Psalm settings has been my greatest joy. In writing these settings, I had a singular goal: to express the words of the Psalmist, meaningfully through the music, with sensitivity to the natural declamation of the text, giving particular emphasis to the depth of expression of both mood and emotion.

These Psalm settings have been successfully and gratefully field-tested at Christ Church. They provided the ultimate litmus test. If the congregation could sing the refrain well, then I kept it! There are a variety of musical styles represented in these settings. There were times when the refrain text cried out for a certain style: sometimes pompous or playful, stark and somber, or serene.

Music not only serves to reflect and amplify the lections of the day, it also gives voice to the soul of the congregation. And in such a task, musicians and composers are called to give the people an avenue of expression. In empowering the people to sing, with vigor and strength, we give them permission to feel. And then we give an opening for the Holy Spirit to move.

Book Contents, Indexes, CD-ROM and Text Sources

The two volumes of the *Portland Psalter,* named for the city within which they were written, contain every Psalm for the Liturgical Years ABC, for both the *Book of Common Prayer Lectionary* (BCP) and the *Revised Common Lectionary* (RCL). Many of the Psalms for Holy Days and Various Occasions are also represented.

The volumes are presented in numerical Psalm order for easy use. Indexes in the back of each volume list liturgical usage for each Psalm according to both the BCP and RCL lectionaries. The second volume will index which Psalm settings are in which volume.

With the publication of the second volume in 2003 comes a CD-ROM with all of the music available electronically. The CD-ROM will be an excellent resource for service bulletins.

The texts in these two volumes come from the Book of Common Prayer, 1979. The majority of the refrains come from the *Gradual Psalter,* published by Church Publishing Inc. Where no refrain was available in the *Gradual Psalter,* some refrains of the *Revised Common Lectionary* are from the *Plainsong Psalter,* also from Church Publishing.

Performance Notes and Ideas

<u>Patterns of Presentation</u>

When singing the Psalms in this style, I encourage the following pattern of presentation:

- organist/pianist introduces the refrain.
- cantor or choir sings the refrain; congregation repeats.
- cantor or choir sings the verses; congregation sings refrain.
- conclude with refrain following last set of verses.

There are a number of ways to sing the verses:

- cantor with organ/piano accompaniment
- choir in four-parts, *a cappella* or with organ/piano accompaniment.
- cantor with organist filling in chord clusters or handbells.
- a quartet sings the verses.

Psalms are not all laid out in neat two-verse patterns as one would think. There are times when groups of three or four verses, or even one verse, cause the meaning to be made most clear. This can make the singing of the verses a bit tricky, and certainly requires some advance preparation. Here are some guidelines:

1. If there is only one verse before the next refrain, start at the second half of the chant tone, or "B" as indicated in the illustration. *see vs. 1 below*
2. If there are three verses before the next refrain, sing the first half of the chant tone twice, before singing the second half on the third verse. (AAB) *see vss. 4-6 below*
3. The chant tone is divided into four sections, two sections before the first double bar and two sections following. If there are four verses (rarely) before the next refrain, use one section of chant tone for each verse. *see Psalm 40, page 30*
4. Some Psalm settings have only groupings of three verses. In those cases, three sections of chant tone are given, so no repetition is necessary. (ABC) *see Psalm 46, page 34*

| Reciting tone |

Here is an illustration of Psalm 146. Chant tone and text are shown with the labels A and B to demonstrate how the Psalm verses are used. As you see, Psalm 146 uses three different verse patterns!

1 **B**   Hallelujah!
Praise the Lord, <u>O my soul!</u> *
     I will praise the Lord as long as I live;
     I will sing praises to my God <u>while I</u>
     <u>have my being.</u>
                 Refrain

2 **A**   Put not your trust in rulers, nor in any
     <u>child of earth</u>, *
     for there <u>is no help in them.</u>

3 **B**   When they breathe their last, they
     re- <u>turn to earth</u>, *
     and in that <u>day their thoughts perish.</u>
                 Refrain

4 **A**   Happy are they who have the God of Jacob
     <u>for their help!</u> *
     whose hope is in <u>the Lord their God;</u>

5 **A**   Who made heaven and earth, the seas, and
     all <u>that is in them;</u> *
     who keeps <u>his promise for ever;</u>

6 **B**   Who gives justice to those who <u>are oppressed,</u> *
     and <u>food to those who hunger.</u>   *Refrain*

Additionally, the pointing is given as an example of how to point the Psalm verses.

Sing the text on the reciting tone until you come to the underlined words, which are the cadence.

Pointing

Pointing is the process of determining how to apply the text of the Psalm to the given chant tones, where to sing on the reciting tone, and when to begin the cadence.

Everyone has a particular way of pointing the Psalms. Take the time to train your cantors to point Psalms sensibly. I teach workshops to my congregation and choirs. I even teach my children's choirs how to point by assigning them Psalms without pointing. Then we talk it through, giving correction as needed. Learning to point takes a little time, but the benefit of knowing will strengthen your cantors and give them greater skill.

Most importantly, pointing should follow natural speech patterns. If there is a single-note cadence, you may want to move on the last word of the line. However, some texts are best pointed so the cadence occurs on the last *accented* word, for example:

Psalm 23:3	He revives my <u>soul</u> *
	    and guides me along right pathways for his <u>Name's sake</u>.
	  NOT for his Name's <u>sake</u>.

Psalm 90:7	For we consume away in your dis<u>pleasure</u>; *
	    we are afraid because of your wrathful indig<u>nation</u>.
	  NOT <u>displeasure</u> or <u>indignation</u>

Psalm 33:15	He fashions all the <u>hearts of them</u> * **NOT** all the hearts of <u>them</u>!

Tempos, Text and Layout

I have given tempo markings for each setting. The markings will give you a sense of the character of each refrain. Keep in mind your acoustics and the skill of your cantor and congregation. The markings are not intended to be a straitjacket, but a helpful reference.

It should be noted that when the text of the refrain matches a complete verse of the Psalm word for word, the verse is omitted from the cantor's text. The exceptions are a few psalms where the text falls within a grouping that would make its deletion awkward. Hence if a verse appears to be missing from the text, it is the refrain.

For some Psalms, the volume of text is sufficient to require that the text layout continue across the bottom from the left to the right page.

Text Declamation

Most importantly, let the text be heard and understood! Train your cantors to express the Psalm conversationally, not sing-song or monotoned, nor overly dramatic. Train them to understand that natural-sounding speech inflection is accomplished through purposeful word accent and timely preparation!

Be adventurous! As an example, the chant line for the verses of Psalm 22, *My God, my God, why have you forsaken me,* is on a single tone. As written, the verse is intense and austere. I have sung this chant line, randomly moving by half-steps in either direction to give the text a haunting and intensely emotional line. For accompaniment, our organist, Christopher Dazey, plays dark, brooding cluster chords, changing registration at each verse. Both presentations are effective. It is possible to paint outside the box. Use the registration of the organ to give color and texture to the verses. Don't get stuck on just one registration for the organ! Use your imagination to bring the Psalms to life.

Permission for Copying and Congregational Use

Purchase of this volume carries with it an authorization for congregations to reproduce in service leaflets either the refrain or the entire setting, as appropriate, as long as the following copyright notice is included on each copy:

Commercial reproduction, or reproduction for sale, of any portion of this psalter without permission of the copyright owner is expressly prohibited. Any questions about appropriate use of permission for commercial reproduction should be addressed to Church Publishing Incorporated, copyrights@cpg.org.

Acknowledgments

Let them praise the Name of the Lord,
for his Name only is exalted,
his splendor is over earth and heaven.
(Psalm 148:13)

This has been a long and fruitful journey. My thanks to the clergy and members of Christ Church who have supported me and provided opportunity for composing, especially the Reverend Shannon P. Leach and the Reverend Jeffrey Bullock. Thanks to the Reverend Dr. Clay Morris for his assistance in this project. Thanks to my music colleagues, Ward Nelson, Scot Crandal, Matthew Penning, Cindy Moore and Christopher Dazey, who have given me sound musical feedback and encouragement. I am grateful to Marilyn Haskel and Frank Tedeschi for providing wise and able guidance through the production of this project; Amy Davis for technical and production assistance; and to the Reverend Dr. John Hooker for excellent editing, proofreading and critique.

Special thanks to my beloved wife, Wendy, for her unwavering support of my work.

Robert A. Hawthorne
Portland, Oregon
                                                                          August, 2002

Proper 25A, Easter 7B, Proper 20B, Epiphany 6C, Proper 1C, Proper 18C

Proper 25A, Epiphany 6C, Proper 1C, Proper 18C

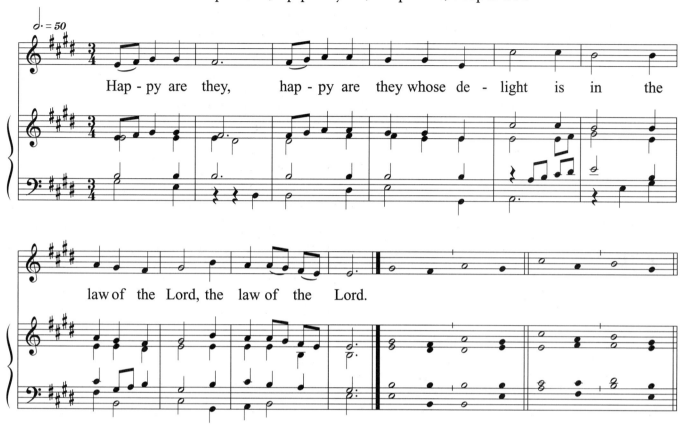

1 Happy are they who have not walked in the counsel of the wicked, *
> nor lingered in the way of sinners,
> nor sat in the seats of the scornful!

2 Their delight is in the law of the Lord, *
> and they meditate on his law day and night. *Refrain*

3 They are like trees planted by streams of water, bearing fruit in due season, with leaves that do not wither; *
> everything they do shall prosper.

4 It is not so with the wicked; *
> they are like chaff which the wind blows away. *Refrain*

5 Therefore the wicked shall not stand upright when judgment comes, *
> nor the sinner in the council of the righteous.

6 For the Lord knows the way of the righteous, *
> but the way of the wicked is doomed. *Refrain*

Psalm 8

RCL Psalm 8

BCP Psalm 8

Holy Name ABC, New Year's Day ABC,
Trinity Sunday AC, Proper 22B

Holy Name ABC, Proper 22B

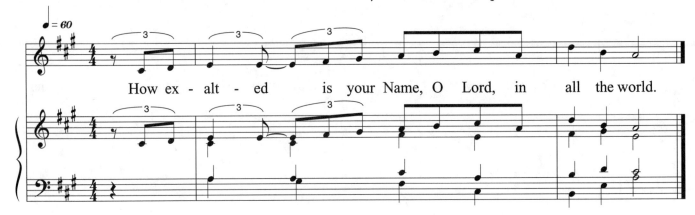

How ex - alt - ed is your Name, O Lord, in all the world.

1 O Lord our Governor, *
    how exalted is your Name in all the
    world!

2 Out of the mouths of infants and children *
    your majesty is praised above the
    heavens.

3 You have set up a stronghold against
your adversaries, *
    to quell the enemy and the avenger.
                                    Refrain

4 When I consider your heavens, the work of
your fingers, *
    the moon and the stars you have set in
    their courses,

5 What is man that you should be
mindful of him? *
    the son of man that you should seek
    him out?   *Refrain*

6 You have made him but little lower than
the angels; *
    you adorn him with glory and honor;

7 You give him mastery over the works of
your hands; *
    you put all things under his feet:
                                    Refrain

8 All sheep and oxen, *
    even the wild beasts of the field,

9 The birds of the air, the fish of the sea, *
    and whatsoever walks in the paths
    of the sea.

10 O Lord our Governor, *
    how exalted is your Name in all the
    world!   *Refrain*

1 How long, O Lord?
   will you forget me for ever? *
       how long will you hide your face
       from me?
2 How long shall I have perplexity in my mind,
   and grief in my heart, day after day? *
       how long shall my enemy triumph
       over me?   *Refrain*

3 Look upon me and answer me,
   O Lord my God; *
       give light to my eyes, lest I sleep in death;
4 Lest my enemy say,
   "I have prevailed over him," *
       and my foes rejoice that I have fallen.
                                         Refrain

5 But I put my trust in your mercy; *
       my heart is joyful because of
       your saving help.
6 I will sing to the Lord,
   for he has dealt with me richly; *
       I will praise the Name of the Lord
       Most High.   *Refrain*

Psalm 15

The right-eous shall a-bide up-on God's ho-ly hill.

1   Lord, who may dwell in your tabernacle? *
     who may abide upon your holy hill?

2   Whoever leads a blameless life and
   does what is right, *
     who speaks the truth from his heart.
                 Refrain

3   There is no guile upon his tongue;
   he does no evil to his friend; *
     he does not heap contempt upon his
     neighbor.

4   In his sight the wicked is rejected, *
     but he honors those who fear the Lord.
                 Refrain

5   He has sworn to do no wrong *
     and does not take back his word.

6   He does not give his money in
   hope of gain, *
     nor does he take a bribe against the
     innocent.   *Refrain*

7   Whoever does these things *
     shall never be overthrown.   *Refrain*

The Lord will show you the path of life.

1   Protect me, O God, for I take
refuge in you; *
>   I have said to the Lord, "You are
>   my Lord, my good above all other."

2   All my delight is upon the godly that are
in the land, *
>   upon those who are noble among
>   the people.   *Refrain*

3   But those who run after other gods *
>   shall have their troubles multiplied.

4   Their libations of blood I will not offer, *
>   nor take the names of their gods
>   upon my lips.   *Refrain*

5   O Lord, you are my portion and my cup; *
>   it is you who uphold my lot.

6   My boundaries enclose a pleasant land; *
>   indeed, I have a goodly heritage.
>   *Refrain*

7   I will bless the Lord who gives me counsel; *
>   my heart teaches me, night after night.

8   I have set the Lord always before me; *
>   because he is at my right hand I
>   shall not fall.   *Refrain*

9   My heart, therefore, is glad, and my
spirit rejoices; *
>   my body also shall rest in hope.

10   For you will not abandon me to the grave, *
>   nor let your holy one see the Pit.
>   *Refrain*

11   You will show me the path of life; *
>   in your presence there is fullness of joy,
>   and in your right hand are pleasures
>   for evermore.   *Refrain*

Psalm 19

RCL Psalm 19   Lent 3B
BCP Psalm 19:7-14   Lent 3B

(Let the words)

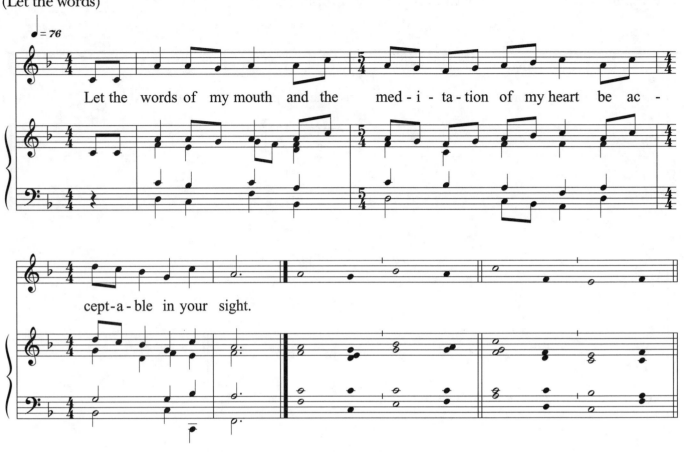

Let the words of my mouth and the med-i-ta-tion of my heart be ac-cept-a-ble in your sight.

1 The heavens declare the glory of God, *
    and the firmament shows his
    handiwork.

2 One day tells its tale to another, *
    and one night imparts knowledge to
    another.   *Refrain*

3 Although they have no words or language, *
    and their voices are not heard,

4 Their sound has gone out into all lands, *
    and their message to the ends of
    the world.   *Refrain*

5 In the deep has he set a pavilion for
the sun; *
    it comes forth like a bridegroom out of
    his chamber; it rejoices like a champion
    to run its course.

6 It goes forth from the uttermost edge of
the heavens and runs about to the end of it
again; *
    nothing is hidden from its burning heat.
    Refrain

Text continues on next page

RCL Psalm 19   Easter Vigil ABC, Proper 22A, Proper 19B,
RCL Psalm 19:7-14   Proper 21B
BCP Psalm 19:7-14   Proper 21B

Psalm 19

(The statutes of the Lord)

7 The law of the Lord is perfect
and revives the soul; *
    the testimony of the Lord is sure
    and gives wisdom to the innocent.

8 The statutes of the Lord are just
and rejoice the heart; *
    the commandment of the Lord is clear
    and gives light to the eyes.   *Refrain*

9 The fear of the Lord is clean
and endures for ever; *
    the judgments of the Lord are true
    and righteous altogether.

10 More to be desired are they than gold,
more than much fine gold, *
    sweeter far than honey,
    than honey in the comb.   *Refrain*

11 By them also is your servant enlightened, *
    and in keeping them there is great
    reward.

12 Who can tell how often he offends? *
    cleanse me from my secret faults.   *Refrain*

13 Above all, keep your servant from
presumptuous sins; let them not get
dominion over me; *
    then shall I be whole and sound,
    and innocent of a great offense.

14 Let the words of my mouth and the
meditation of my heart be acceptable in
your sight, *
    O Lord, my strength and my redeemer.
                    Refrain

Psalm 22

(My God, my God)

RCL Psalm 22 — Good Friday ABC
BCP Psalm 22:1-21 — Good Friday ABC, Palm Sunday: Eucharist ABC
BCP Psalm 22:1-11 — Good Friday ABC, Palm Sunday: Eucharist ABC

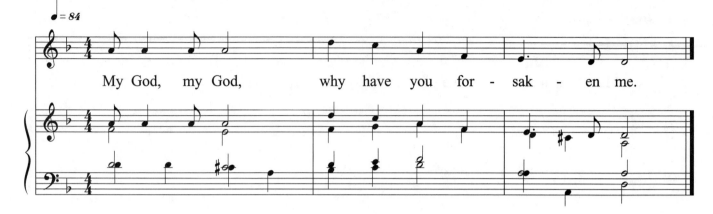

My God, my God, why have you for - sak - en me.

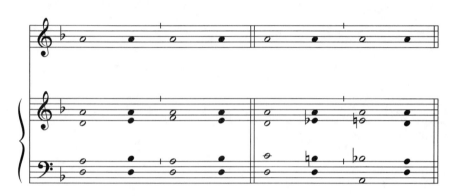

1   My God, my God, why have you
    forsaken me? *
        and are so far from my cry
        and from the words of my distress?
2   O my God, I cry in the daytime, but you
    do not answer; *
        by night as well, but I find no rest.
                                        Refrain
3   Yet you are the Holy One, *
        enthroned upon the praises of Israel.
4   Our forefathers put their trust in you; *
        they trusted, and you delivered them.
5   They cried out to you and were delivered; *
        they trusted in you and were not
        put to shame.   *Refrain*

6   But as for me, I am a worm and no man, *
        scorned by all and despised by
        the people.
7   All who see me laugh me to scorn; *
        they curl their lips and wag their
        heads, saying,
8   "He trusted in the Lord; let him deliver him; *
        let him rescue him, if he
        delights in him."   *Refrain*

9   Yet you are he who took me out of the womb, *
        and kept me safe upon my mother's breast.
10 I have been entrusted to you ever since I was
    born; *
        you were my God when I was still in my
        mother's womb.
11 Be not far from me, for trouble is near, *
        and there is none to help.   *Refrain*

12 Many young bulls encircle me; *
        strong bulls of Bashan surround me.
13 They open wide their jaws at me, *
        like a ravening and a roaring lion.
                                        Refrain
14 I am poured out like water;
    all my bones are out of joint; *
        my heart within my breast is melting wax.
15 My mouth is dried out like a pot-sherd;
    my tongue sticks to the roof of my mouth; *
        and you have laid me in the dust of
        the grave.   *Refrain*

16 Packs of dogs close me in,
    and gangs of evildoers circle around me; *
        they pierce my hands and my feet;
        I can count all my bones.

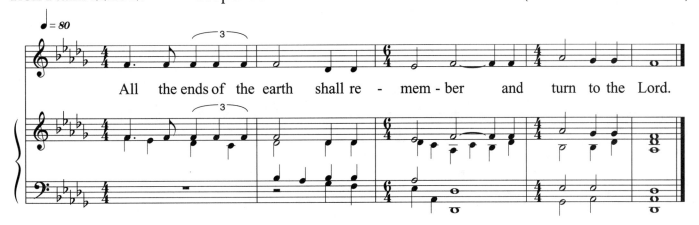

17 They stare and gloat over me; *
       they divide my garments among them;
       they cast lots for my clothing.   *Refrain*

18 Be not far away, O Lord; *
       you are my strength; hasten to help me.

19 Save me from the sword, *
       my life from the power of the dog.   *Refrain*

20 Save me from the lion's mouth, *
       my wretched body from the horns of
       wild bulls.

21 I will declare your Name to my brethren; *
       in the midst of the congregation I will
       praise you.   *Refrain*

22 Praise the Lord, you that fear him; *
       stand in awe of him, O offspring of
       Israel; all you of Jacob's line, give glory.

23 For he does not despise nor abhor the
   poor in their poverty; neither does he hide
   his face from them; *
       but when they cry to him he
       hears them.   *Refrain*

24 My praise is of him in the great assembly; *
       I will perform my vows in the presence of
       those who worship him.

25 The poor shall eat and be satisfied,
   and those who seek the Lord shall praise him: *
       "May your heart live for ever!"   *Refrain*

26 All the ends of the earth shall remember and
   turn to the Lord, *
       and all the families of the nations shall
       bow before him.

27 For kingship belongs to the Lord; *
       he rules over the nations.   *Refrain*

28 To him alone all who sleep in the earth bow
   down in worship; *
       all who go down to the dust fall
       before him.

29 My soul shall live for him;
   my descendants shall serve him; *
       they shall be known as the Lord's for ever.

30 They shall come and make known to a
   people yet unborn *
       the saving deeds that he has done.
                                           Refrain

Psalm 23

RCL Psalm 23   Lent 4A, Easter 4ABC, Proper 11C
BCP Psalm 23   Lent 4A, Easter 4AB

The Lord is my Shep-herd, I shall not be in want.

2   He makes me lie down in green pastures *
     and leads me beside still waters.

3   He revives my soul *
     and guides me along right pathways for
     his Name's sake.   *Refrain*

4   Though I walk through the valley of the
    shadow of death, I shall fear no evil; *
     for you are with me;
     your rod and your staff,
     they comfort me.

5   You spread a table before me in the
    presence of those who trouble me; *
     you have anointed my head with oil,
     and my cup is running over.   *Refrain*

6   Surely your goodness and mercy shall
    follow me all the days of my life, *
     and I will dwell in the house of the
     Lord for ever.   *Refrain*

1 The earth is the Lord's and all that is in it, *
    the world and all who dwell therein.
2 For it is he who founded it upon the seas *
    and made it firm upon the rivers of the
    deep.   *Refrain*

3 "Who can ascend the hill of the Lord? *
    and who can stand in his holy place?"
4 "Those who have clean hands and
   a pure heart, *
    who have not pledged themselves to
    falsehood, nor sworn by what is a
    fraud.   *Refrain*

5 They shall receive a blessing from the Lord *
    and a just reward from the God of
    their salvation."
6 Such is the generation of those who seek
   him, *
    of those who seek your face,
    O God of Jacob.   *Refrain*

7 Lift up your heads, O gates;
   lift them high, O everlasting doors; *
    and the King of glory shall come in.
8 "Who is this King of glory?" *
    "The Lord, strong and mighty,
    the Lord, mighty in battle."   *Refrain*

9 Lift up your heads, O gates;
   lift them high, O everlasting doors; *
    and the King of glory shall come in.
10 "Who is he, this King of glory?" *
    "The Lord of hosts,
    he is the King of glory."   *Refrain*

Psalm 25

RCL Psalm 25:1-9   Lent 1B
BCP Psalm 25:3-9   Lent 1B

Lead me in your truth, O Lord and teach me.

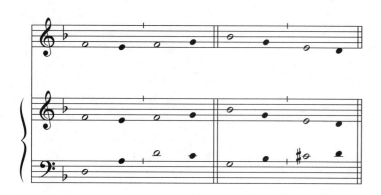

1 To you, O Lord, I lift up my soul;
  my God, I put my trust in you; *
      let me not be humiliated,
  nor let my enemies triumph over me.

2 Let none who look to you be put to shame; *
      let the treacherous be disappointed in
      their schemes.   *Refrain*

3 Show me your ways, O Lord, *
      and teach me your paths.

4 Lead me in your truth and teach me, *
      for you are the God of my salvation;
      in you have I trusted all the day long.
                       Refrain

5 Remember, O Lord, your compassion and
  love, *
      for they are from everlasting.

6 Remember not the sins of my youth and
  my transgressions; *
      remember me according to your love
      and for the sake of your goodness, O
      Lord.   *Refrain*

7 Gracious and upright is the Lord; *
      therefore he teaches sinners in his way.

8 He guides the humble in doing right *
      and teaches his way to the lowly.

9 All the paths of the Lord are love
  and faithfulness *
      to those who keep his covenant and his
      testimonies.   *Refrain*

Page has been left blank
to facilitate page turns.

Psalm 27

RCL Psalm 27:1, 5-13
RCL Psalm 27

Epiphany 3A
Lent 2C

(RCL)

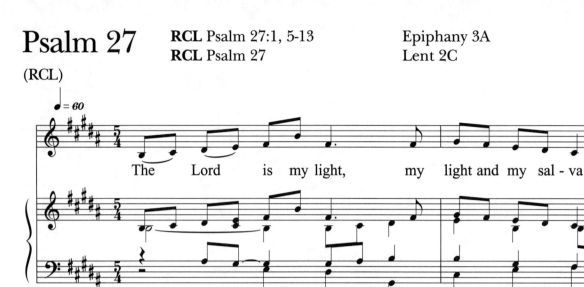

1 The Lord is my light and my salvation;
  whom then shall I fear? *
        the Lord is the strength of my life;
        of whom then shall I be afraid? *Refrain*

2 When evildoers came upon me to eat up
  my flesh, *
        it was they, my foes and my adversaries,
        who stumbled and fell.

3 Though an army should encamp
  against me, *
        yet my heart shall not be afraid;

4 And though war should rise up against me, *
        yet will I put my trust in him. *Refrain*

5 One thing have I asked of the Lord;
  one thing I seek; *
        that I may dwell in the house of the
        Lord all the days of my life;

6 To behold the fair beauty of the Lord *
        and to seek him in his temple. *Refrain*

7 For in the day of trouble he shall keep me
  safe in his shelter; *
        he shall hide me in the secrecy of
        his dwelling and set me high upon a
        rock. *Refrain*

8 Even now he lifts up my head *
        above my enemies round about me.

9 Therefore I will offer in his dwelling an
  oblation with sounds of great gladness; *
        I will sing and make music to the Lord.
        Refrain

10 Hearken to my voice, O Lord, when I call; *
        have mercy on me and answer me.

11 You speak in my heart and say,
   "Seek my face." *
        Your face, Lord, will I seek. *Refrain*

Text continues on next page

12 Hide not your face from me, *
    nor turn away your servant in displeasure.

13 You have been my helper; cast me not away; *
    do not forsake me, O God of my salvation.
                                            Refrain

14 Though my father and my mother forsake me, *
    the Lord will sustain me.

15 Show me your way, O Lord; *
    lead me on a level path, because of my enemies.

16 Deliver me not into the hand of my adversaries, *
    for false witnesses have risen up against me,
    and also those who speak malice.
                                            Refrain

17 What if I had not believed
    that I should see the goodness of the Lord *
    in the land of the living!

18 O tarry and await the Lord's pleasure;
    be strong, and he shall comfort your heart; *
    wait patiently for the Lord.   *Refrain*

Psalm 29

Epiphany 1 ABC, Trinity Sunday B

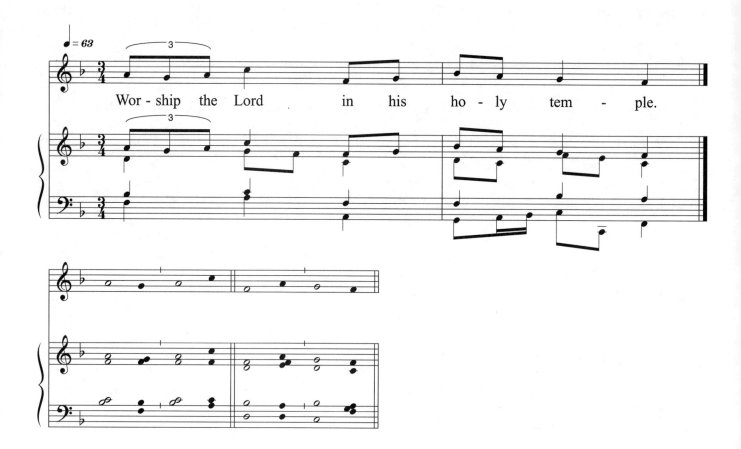

Worship the Lord in his holy temple.

1   Ascribe to the Lord, you gods, *
     ascribe to the Lord glory and strength.
2   Ascribe to the Lord the glory due his
  Name; *
     worship the Lord in the beauty of
     holiness.   *Refrain*
3   The voice of the Lord is upon the waters;
  the God of glory thunders; *
     the Lord is upon the mighty waters.
4   The voice of the Lord is a powerful voice; *
     the voice of the Lord is a voice of
     splendor.   *Refrain*
5   The voice of the Lord breaks the cedar
  trees; *
     the Lord breaks the cedars of
     Lebanon;
6   He makes Lebanon skip like a calf, *
     and Mount Hermon like a young wild
     ox.   *Refrain*

7   The voice of the Lord splits the flames of fire;
  the voice of the Lord shakes the wilderness; *
     the Lord shakes the wilderness
     of Kadesh.   *Refrain*
8   The voice of the Lord makes the oak trees
  writhe *
     and strips the forests bare.
9   And in the temple of the Lord *
     all are crying, "Glory!"   *Refrain*

10   The Lord sits enthroned above the flood; *
      the Lord sits enthroned as King
      for evermore.
11   The Lord shall give strength to his people; *
      the Lord shall give his people the
      blessing of peace.   *Refrain*

RCL Psalm 30

BCP Psalm 30:1-6, 12-13

Epiphany 6B, Proper 1B, Proper 8B, Proper 5C,
Proper 9C

Proper 5C

Psalm 30

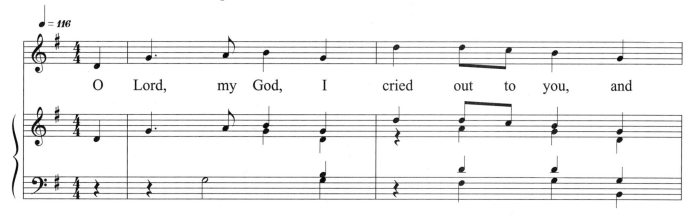

O Lord, my God, I cried out to you, and

you re-stored me to health.

1   I will exalt you, O Lord,
    because you have lifted me up *
            and have not let my enemies triumph
            over me.
2   O Lord my God, I cried out to you, *
            and you restored me to health.   *Refrain*

3   You brought me up, O Lord, from the
    dead; *
            you restored my life as I was going
            down to the grave.
4   Sing to the Lord, you servants of his; *
            give thanks for the remembrance of
            his holiness.   *Refrain*

5   For his wrath endures but the twinkling
    of an eye, *
            his favor for a lifetime.
6   Weeping may spend the night, *
            but joy comes in the morning.   *Refrain*

7   While I felt secure, I said,
    "I shall never be disturbed. *
            You, Lord, with your favor, made me
            as strong as the mountains."
8   Then you hid your face, *
            and I was filled with fear.   *Refrain*

9   I cried to you, O Lord; *
            I pleaded with the Lord, saying,
10 "What profit is there in my blood, if I
    go down to the Pit? *
            will the dust praise you or declare
            your faithfulness?
11 Hear, O Lord, and have mercy upon me; *
            O Lord, be my helper."   *Refrain*

12 You have turned my wailing into dancing; *
            you have put off my sack-cloth
            and clothed me with joy.
13 Therefore my heart sings to you without
    ceasing; *
            O Lord my God, I will give you thanks
            for ever.   *Refrain*

Psalm 31

RCL Psalm 31:1-5, 15-16   Holy Saturday ABC
RCL Psalm 31:9-16   Palm Sunday: Eucharist ABC
BCP Psalm 31:1-5   Holy Saturday ABC

In - to your hands, O Lord, I com - mend my spir - it.

1 In you, O Lord, have I taken refuge;
  let me never be put to shame; *
     deliver me in your righteousness.

2 Incline your ear to me; *
     make haste to deliver me.

3 Be my strong rock, a castle to keep me safe,
  for you are my crag and my stronghold; *
     for the sake of your Name, lead me
     and guide me.   *Refrain*

4 Take me out of the net that they have
  secretly set for me, *
     for you are my tower of strength.

5 Into your hands I commend my spirit, *
     for you have redeemed me,
     O Lord, O God of truth.   *Refrain*

9 Have mercy on me, O Lord, for I am in
  trouble; *
     my eye is consumed with sorrow,
     and also my throat and my belly.

10 For my life is wasted with grief,
  and my years with sighing; *
     my strength fails me because of affliction,
  and my bones are consumed.   *Refrain*

11 I have become a reproach to all my enemies
  and even to my neighbors, a dismay to those
  of my acquaintance; *
     when they see me in the street they
     avoid me.

12 I am forgotten like a dead man, out of mind; *
     I am as useless as a broken pot.   *Refrain*

13 For I have heard the whispering of the crowd;
  fear is all around; *
     they put their heads together against me;
     they plot to take my life.

14 But as for me, I have trusted in you, O Lord. *
     I have said, "You are my God.   *Refrain*

15 My times are in your hand; *
     rescue me from the hand of my enemies,
     and from those who persecute me.

16 Make your face to shine upon your servant, *
     and in your loving-kindness save me."
                           Refrain

Page has been left blank
to facilitate page turns.

Psalm 32

(Happy are they)

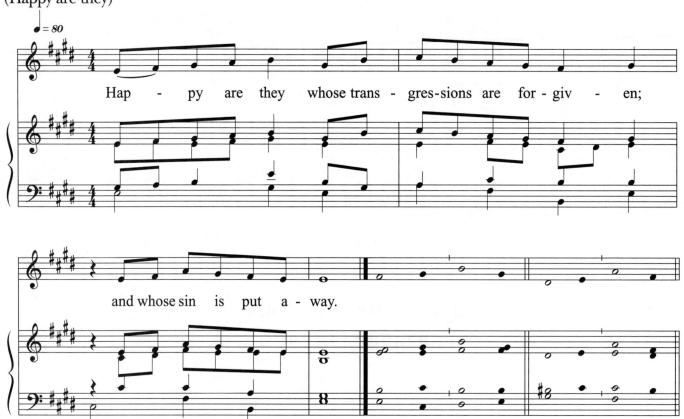

♩ = 80

Hap - py are they whose trans - gres-sions are for - giv - en;

and whose sin is put a - way.

2 Happy are they to whom the Lord
imputes no guilt, *
      and in whose spirit there is no guile!
                           Refrain

3 While I held my tongue, my bones
withered away, *
      because of my groaning all day long.

4 For your hand was heavy upon me
day and night; *
      my moisture was dried up as in the
      heat of summer.   *Refrain*

5 Then I acknowledged my sin to you, *
      and did not conceal my guilt.

6 I said, "I will confess my transgressions
to the Lord." *
      Then you forgave me the guilt of my
      sin.   *Refrain*

7 Therefore all the faithful will make their
prayers to you in time of trouble; *
      when the great waters overflow, they
      shall not reach them.

8 You are my hiding-place;
you preserve me from trouble; *
      you surround me with shouts of
      deliverance.   *Refrain*

9 "I will instruct you and teach you in the way
that you should go; *
      I will guide you with my eye.

10 Do not be like horse or mule, which have
no understanding; *
      who must be fitted with bit and bridle,
      or else they will not stay near you."
                           Refrain

11 Great are the tribulations of the wicked; *
      but mercy embraces those who trust in
      the Lord.

12 Be glad, you righteous, and rejoice in the
Lord; *
      shout for joy, all who are true of heart.
                           Refrain

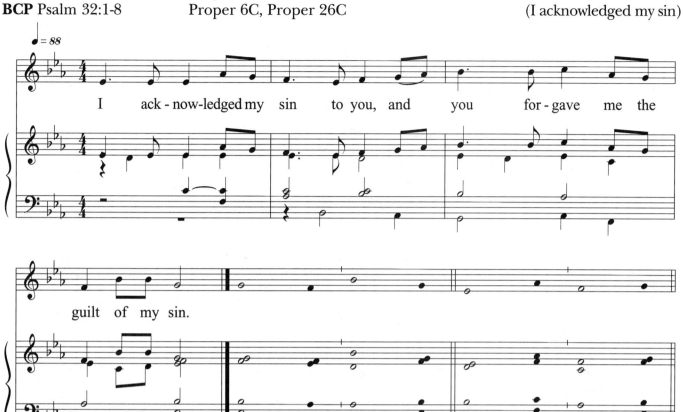

I ack-now-ledged my sin to you, and you for-gave me the guilt of my sin.

1 Happy are they whose transgressions are forgiven, *
    and whose sin is put away!

2 Happy are they to whom the Lord imputes no guilt, *
    and in whose spirit there is no guile!
    Refrain

3 While I held my tongue, my bones withered away, *
    because of my groaning all day long.

4 For your hand was heavy upon me day and night; *
    my moisture was dried up as in the heat of summer.   *Refrain*

5 Then I acknowledged my sin to you, *
    and did not conceal my guilt.

6 I said, "I will confess my transgressions to the Lord." *
    Then you forgave me the guilt of my sin.   *Refrain*

7 Therefore all the faithful will make their prayers to you in time of trouble; *
    when the great waters overflow, they shall not reach them.

8 You are my hiding-place; you preserve me from trouble; *
    you surround me with shouts of deliverance.   *Refrain*

9 "I will instruct you and teach you in the way that you should go; *
    I will guide you with my eye.

10 Do not be like horse or mule, which have no understanding; *
    who must be fitted with bit and bridle, or else they will not stay near you."
    Refrain

11 Great are the tribulations of the wicked; *
    but mercy embraces those who trust in the Lord.

12 Be glad, you righteous, and rejoice in the Lord; *
    shout for joy, all who are true of heart.
    Refrain

Psalm 33

(Sing to the Lord)

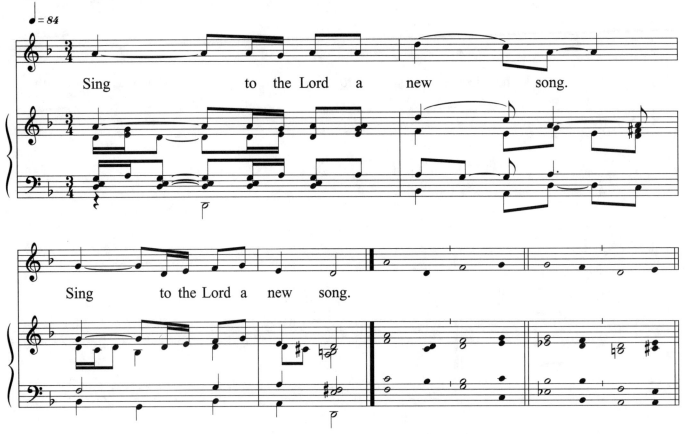

Sing to the Lord a new song.

Sing to the Lord a new song.

1   Rejoice in the Lord, you righteous; *
        it is good for the just to sing praises.
2   Praise the Lord with the harp; *
        play to him upon the psaltery and lyre.
3   Sing for him a new song; *
        sound a fanfare with all your skill
        upon the trumpet.   *Refrain*

4   For the word of the Lord is right, *
        and all his works are sure.
5   He loves righteousness and justice; *
        the loving-kindness of the Lord fills
        the whole earth.   *Refrain*

6   By the word of the Lord were the heavens
    made, *
        by the breath of his mouth all the
        heavenly hosts.
7   He gathers up the waters of the ocean as
    in a water-skin *
        and stores up the depths of the sea.
                                                   Refrain

8   Let all the earth fear the Lord; *
        let all who dwell in the world stand
        in awe of him.
9   For he spoke, and it came to pass; *
        he commanded, and it stood fast.
                                                   Refrain

10 The Lord brings the will of the nations
    to naught; *
        he thwarts the designs of the peoples.
11 But the Lord's will stands fast for ever, *
        and the designs of his heart from
        age to age.   *Refrain*

Psalm 33

(Lord, let your loving-kindness)

Lord, let you lov-ing-kind-ness be up-on us, as

we have put our trust in you.

12 Happy is the nation whose God is the Lord! *
        happy the people he has chosen to
        be his own!
13 The Lord looks down from heaven, *
        and beholds all the people in the
        world.   *Refrain*

14 From where he sits enthroned he turns his
    gaze *
        on all who dwell on the earth.
15 He fashions all the hearts of them *
        and understands all their works.
                                                  Refrain

16 There is no king that can be saved by
    a mighty army; *
        a strong man is not delivered by
        his great strength.
17 The horse is a vain hope for deliverance; *
        for all its strength it cannot save.
                                                  Refrain

18 Behold, the eye of the Lord is upon those
    who fear him, *
        on those who wait upon his love,
19 To pluck their lives from death, *
        and to feed them in time of famine.
                                                  Refrain

20 Our soul waits for the Lord; *
        he is our help and our shield.
21 Indeed, our heart rejoices in him, *
        for in his holy Name we put our trust.
                                                  Refrain

Psalm 33

RCL Psalm 33:12-22 Proper 14C
BCP Psalm 33:12-15, 18-22 Proper 14C

(Our soul waits)

Our soul waits for the Lord; he is our help and our shield.

12 Happy is the nation whose God is the Lord! *
    happy the people he has chosen to
    be his own!
13 The Lord looks down from heaven, *
    and beholds all the people in the
    world. *Refrain*

14 From where he sits enthroned he turns his
gaze *
    on all who dwell on the earth.
15 He fashions all the hearts of them *
    and understands all their works.
                           Refrain

16 There is no king that can be saved by
a mighty army; *
    a strong man is not delivered by
    his great strength.
17 The horse is a vain hope for deliverance; *
    for all its strength it cannot save.
                           Refrain

18 Behold, the eye of the Lord is upon those
who fear him, *
    on those who wait upon his love,
19 To pluck their lives from death, *
    and to feed them in time of famine.
                           Refrain
21 Indeed, our heart rejoices in him, *
    for in his holy Name we put our trust.
22 Let your loving-kindness, O Lord, be
upon us, *
    as we have put our trust in you. *Refrain*

Page has been left blank
to facilitate page turns.

Psalm 34

(vss. 1-10, 19-22)

RCL Psalm 34:1-10, 22	All Saints' Day A
RCL Psalm 34:1-8	Proper 14B
RCL Psalm 34:1-8 (19-22)	Proper 25B
BCP Psalm 34:1-8	Proper 14B, Lent 4C

Taste and see that the Lord is good; taste and see, taste and see.

1 I will bless the Lord at all times; *
    his praise shall ever be in my mouth.
2 I will glory in the Lord; *
    let the humble hear and rejoice.
                                    Refrain

3 Proclaim with me the greatness of the
    Lord; *
    let us exalt his Name together.
4 I sought the Lord, and he answered me *
    and delivered me out of all my terror.
                                    Refrain

5 Look upon him and be radiant, *
    and let not your faces be ashamed.
6 I called in my affliction and the
    Lord heard me *
    and saved me from all my troubles.
                                    Refrain

7 The angel of the Lord encompasses those
    who fear him, *
    and he will deliver them.
8 Taste and see that the Lord is good; *
    happy are they who trust in him!
                                    Refrain

9 Fear the Lord, you that are his saints, *
    for those who fear him lack nothing.
10 The young lions lack and suffer hunger, *
    but those who seek the Lord lack
    nothing that is good.   *Refrain*

19 Many are the troubles of the righteous, *
    but the Lord will deliver him out of them
    all.
20 He will keep safe all his bones; *
    not one of them shall be broken.
                                    Refrain

21 Evil shall slay the wicked, *
    and those who hate the righteous
    will be punished.
22 The Lord ransoms the life of his servants, *
    and none will be punished who trust in him.
                                    Refrain

RCL Psalm 34:9-14   Proper 15B
RCL Psalm 34:15-22   Proper 16B
BCP Psalm 34:9-14   Proper 15B
BCP Psalm 34:15-22   Proper 16B

(vss. 9-14, 15-22)

Taste and see that the Lord is good; taste and see, taste and see.

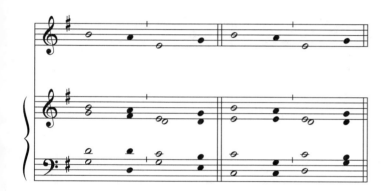

9   Fear the Lord, you that are his saints, *
     for those who fear him lack nothing.

10 The young lions lack and suffer hunger, *
     but those who seek the Lord lack
     nothing that is good.   *Refrain*

11 Come, children, and listen to me; *
     I will teach you the fear of the Lord.

12 Who among you loves life *
     and desires long life to enjoy prosperity?
             Refrain

13 Keep your tongue from evil-speaking *
     and your lips from lying words.

14 Turn from evil and do good; *
     seek peace and pursue it.   *Refrain*

15 The eyes of the Lord are upon the
    righteous, *
     and his ears are open to their cry.

16 The face of the Lord is against those who
    do evil, *
     to root out the remembrance of them
     from the earth.   *Refrain*

17 The righteous cry, and the Lord hears them *
     and delivers them from all their troubles.

18 The Lord is near to the brokenhearted *
     and will save those whose spirits
     are crushed.   *Refrain*

19 Many are the troubles of the righteous, *
     but the Lord will deliver him out of them
     all.

20 He will keep safe all his bones; *
     not one of them shall be broken.
             Refrain

21 Evil shall slay the wicked, *
     and those who hate the righteous
     will be punished.

22 The Lord ransoms the life of his servants, *
     and none will be punished who trust in
     him.   *Refrain*

Psalm 37

(RCL)

RCL Psalm 37:1-12, 41-42   Epiphany 7C
RCL Psalm 37:1-18   Proper 2C
RCL Psalm 37:1-10   Proper 22C

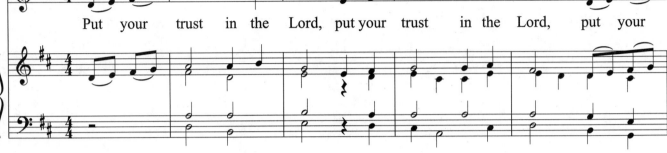

Put your trust in the Lord, put your trust in the Lord, put your

trust in the Lord and do good.

1   Do not fret yourself because of evildoers; *
    do not be jealous of those who
    do wrong.
2   For they shall soon wither like the grass, *
    and like the green grass fade away.
Refrain
3   Put your trust in the Lord and do good; *
    dwell in the land and feed on its riches.
4   Take delight in the Lord, *
    and he shall give you your heart's desire.
Refrain
5   Commit your way to the Lord and put your
    trust in him, *
    and he will bring it to pass.
6   He will make your righteousness as
    clear as the light *
    and your just dealing as the noonday.
Refrain

7   Be still before the Lord *
    and wait patiently for him.
8   Do not fret yourself over the one who prospers, *
    the one who succeeds in evil schemes.
Refrain
9   Refrain from anger, leave rage alone; *
    do not fret yourself; it leads only to evil.
10   For evildoers shall be cut off, *
    but those who wait upon the Lord
    shall possess the land.   *Refrain*

11   In a little while the wicked shall be no more; *
    you shall search out their place, but
    they will not be there.
12   But the lowly shall possess the land; *
    they will delight in abundance of peace.
Refrain

Text continues on next page

BCP Psalm 37:1-6
BCP Psalm 37:1-18
BCP Psalm 37:3-10

Epiphany 4A
Epiphany 4A, Epiphany 7C, Proper 2C, Proper 22C
Epiphany 4A, Epiphany 7C, Proper 2C, Proper 22C

Psalm 37
(BCP)

Put your trust in the Lord, put your trust in the Lord, put your

trust in the Lord and do good.

13 The wicked plot against the righteous *
        and gnash at them with their teeth.
14 The Lord laughs at the wicked, *
        because he sees that their day will
        come.   *Refrain*

15 The wicked draw their sword and bend
    their bow to strike down the poor and
    needy, *
        to slaughter those who are upright in
        their ways.
16 Their sword shall go through their own
    heart, *
        and their bow shall be broken.   *Refrain*

17 The little that the righteous has *
        is better than great riches of the
        wicked.
18 For the power of the wicked shall be
    broken, *
        but the Lord upholds the righteous.
                                    Refrain

41 But the deliverance of the righteous
    comes from the Lord; *
        he is their stronghold in time of trouble.
42 The Lord will help them and rescue them; *
        he will rescue them from the wicked
        and deliver them, because they
        seek refuge in him.   *Refrain*

Psalm 40

RCL Psalm 40:1-12   Epiphany 2A
BCP Psalm 40:1-10   Epiphany 2A

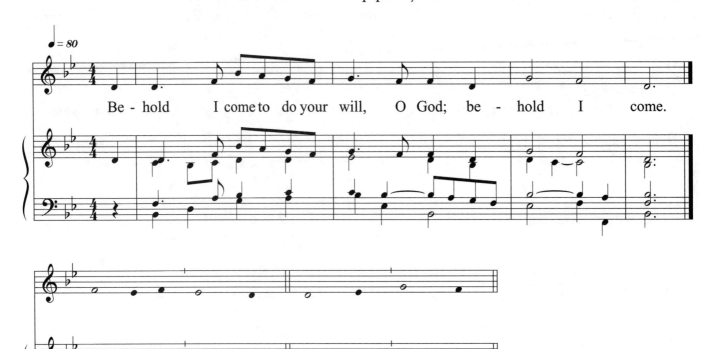

Be - hold   I come to do your will,   O God; be - hold   I   come.

1   I waited patiently upon the Lord; *
    he stooped to me and heard my cry.
2   He lifted me out of the desolate pit, out of
the mire and clay; *
    he set my feet upon a high cliff and
    made my footing sure.
3   He put a new song in my mouth,
a song of praise to our God; *
    many shall see, and stand in awe,
    and put their trust in the Lord.
4   Happy are they who trust in the Lord! *
    they do not resort to evil spirits or turn
    to false gods.   *Refrain*

5   Great things are they that you have done,
O Lord my God! how great your wonders
and your plans for us! *
    there is none who can be compared
    with you.
6   Oh, that I could make them known
and tell them! *
    but they are more than I can count.

7   In sacrifice and offering you take no pleasure *
    (you have given me ears to hear you);
8   Burnt-offering and sin-offering you
have not required, *
    and so I said, "Behold, I come.   *Refrain*
9   In the roll of the book it is written
concerning me: *
    'I love to do your will, O my God;
    your law is deep in my heart.'"
10 I proclaimed righteousness in the
great congregation; *
    behold, I did not restrain my lips;
    and that, O Lord, you know.   *Refrain*
11 Your righteousness have I not hidden in my
heart; I have spoken of your faithfulness and
your deliverance; *
    I have not concealed your love and
    faithfulness from the great congregation.
12 You are the Lord;
do not withhold your compassion from me; *
    let your love and your faithfulness
    keep me safe for ever.   *Refrain*

1 Happy are they who consider the
poor and needy! *
     the Lord will deliver them in the
     time of trouble.

2 The Lord preserves them and keeps them
alive, so that they may be happy in the land; *
     he does not hand them over to the
     will of their enemies.

3 The Lord sustains them on their sickbed *
     and ministers to them in their illness.
                                          Refrain

4 I said, "Lord, be merciful to me; *
     heal me, for I have sinned against you."

5 My enemies are saying wicked things
about me: *
     "When will he die, and his name
     perish?"   *Refrain*

6 Even if they come to see me, they
speak empty words; *
     their heart collects false rumors;
     they go outside and spread them.

7 All my enemies whisper together about me *
     and devise evil against me.

8 "A deadly thing," they say, "has
fastened on him; *
     he has taken to his bed and will
     never get up again."   *Refrain*

9 Even my best friend, whom I trusted,
who broke bread with me, *
     has lifted up his heel and turned
     against me.

10 But you, O Lord, be merciful to me and
raise me up, *
     and I shall repay them.

11 By this I know you are pleased with me, *
     that my enemy does not triumph over me.
                                          Refrain

12 In my integrity you hold me fast, *
     and shall set me before your face for ever.

13 Blessed be the Lord God of Israel, *
     from age to age. Amen. Amen.   *Refrain*

Psalm 42

RCL Psalm 42   Easter Vigil ABC
RCL Psalm 42   Proper 7C
BCP Psalm 42:1-7   Easter Vigil ABC
BCP Psalm 42; 42:1-7   Epiphany 6B, Proper 1B

As the deer longs for the wa-ter-brooks, so longs my soul for you, O God.

2   My soul is athirst for God, athirst for
the living God; *
     when shall I come to appear before the
     presence of God?

3   My tears have been my food day and night, *
     while all day long they say to me,
     "Where now is your God?"   *Refrain*

4   I pour out my soul when I think on these
things: *
     how I went with the multitude and led
     them into the house of God,

5   With the voice of praise and thanksgiving, *
     among those who keep holy-day. *Refrain*

6   Why are you so full of heaviness, O my soul? *
     and why are you so disquieted within me?

7   Put your trust in God; *
     for I will yet give thanks to him,
     who is the help of my countenance,
     and my God.   *Refrain*

8   My soul is heavy within me; *
     therefore I will remember you from
     the land of Jordan, and from the peak
     of Mizar among the heights of Hermon.

9   One deep calls to another in the noise of
your cataracts; *
     all your rapids and floods have gone over me.
     Refrain

10   The Lord grants his loving-kindness in the
daytime; *
     in the night season his song is with me,
     a prayer to the God of my life.

11   I will say to the God of my strength,
"Why have you forgotten me? *
     and why do I go so heavily while the
     enemy oppresses me?"   *Refrain*

12   While my bones are being broken, *
     my enemies mock me to my face;

13   All day long they mock me *
     and say to me, "Where now is your God?"
     Refrain

14   Why are you so full of heaviness, O my soul? *
     and why are you so disquieted within me?

15   Put your trust in God; *
     for I will yet give thanks to him,
     who is the help of my countenance,
     and my God.   *Refrain*

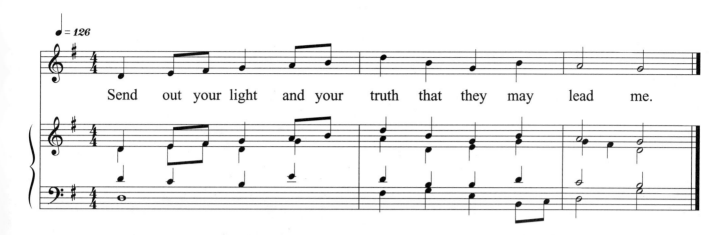

Send out your light and your truth that they may lead me.

1 Give judgment for me, O God,
   and defend my cause against an
   ungodly people; *
       deliver me from the deceitful and
       the wicked.
2 For you are the God of my strength;
   why have you put me from you? *
       and why do I go so heavily while
       the enemy oppresses me?   *Refrain*

3 Send out your light and your truth, that
   they may lead me, *
       and bring me to your holy hill
       and to your dwelling;
4 That I may go to the altar of God,
   to the God of my joy and gladness; *
       and on the harp I will give thanks to
       you, O God my God.   *Refrain*

5 Why are you so full of heaviness, O my soul? *
       and why are you so disquieted within me?
6 Put your trust in God; *
       for I will yet give thanks to him,
       who is the help of my countenance,
       and my God.   *Refrain*

Psalm 46

RCL Psalm 46
BCP Psalm 46

Easter Vigil ABC, Proper 4A, Proper 29C
Easter Vigil ABC, Proper 16C, Proper 29C

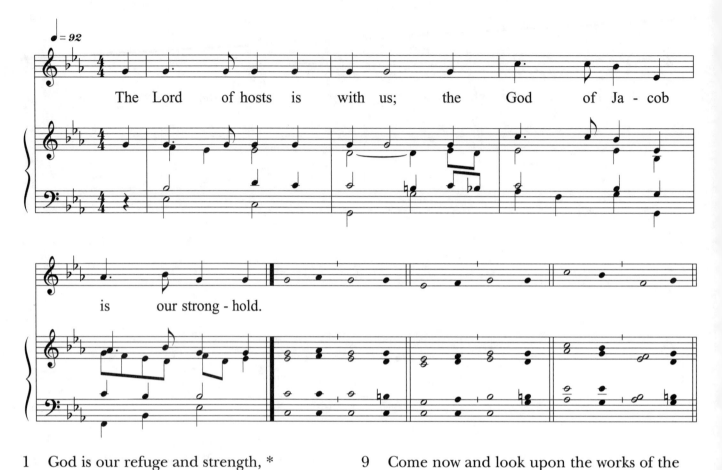

The Lord of hosts is with us; the God of Ja - cob

is our strong - hold.

1   God is our refuge and strength, *
    a very present help in trouble.

2   Therefore we will not fear, though
the earth be moved, *
    and though the mountains be
    toppled into the depths of the sea;

3   Though its waters rage and foam, *
    and though the mountains tremble
    at its tumult.   *Refrain*

5   There is a river whose streams make glad
the city of God, *
    the holy habitation of the Most High.

6   God is in the midst of her;
she shall not be overthrown; *
    God shall help her at the break of day.

7   The nations make much ado, and the
kingdoms are shaken; *
    God has spoken, and the earth
    shall melt away.   *Refrain*

9   Come now and look upon the works of the
Lord, *
    what awesome things he has done on
    earth.

10 It is he who makes war to cease in
all the world; *
    he breaks the bow, and shatters the spear,
    and burns the shields with fire.

11 "Be still, then, and know that I am God; *
    I will be exalted among the nations;
    I will be exalted in the earth."   *Refrain*

RCL Psalm 47   Ascension Day ABC, Easter 7 ABC
BCP Psalm 47   Ascension Day ABC, Easter 7 ABC

God has gone up, has gone up with a shout, the Lord with the sound of the ram's horn.

1   Clap your hands, all you peoples; *
     shout to God with a cry of joy.
2   For the Lord Most High is to be feared; *
     he is the great King over all the earth.
          Refrain

3   He subdues the peoples under us, *
     and the nations under our feet.
4   He chooses our inheritance for us, *
     the pride of Jacob whom he loves.
          Refrain

6   Sing praises to God, sing praises; *
     sing praises to our King, sing praises.
7   For God is King of all the earth; *
     sing praises with all your skill.   *Refrain*

8   God reigns over the nations; *
     God sits upon his holy throne.
9   The nobles of the peoples have
gathered together *
     with the people of the God of Abraham.
10   The rulers of the earth belong to God, *
     and he is highly exalted.   *Refrain*

Psalm 49

RCL Psalm 49:1-11   Proper 13C
BCP Psalm 49:1-11   Proper 13C

We can ne - ver ran - som our - selves, or de - li - ver to God the

price of our life.

1 Hear this, all you peoples;
hearken, all you who dwell in the world, *
  you of high degree and low,
  rich and poor together.

2 My mouth shall speak of wisdom, *
  and my heart shall meditate
  on understanding.

3 I will incline my ear to a proverb *
  and set forth my riddle upon the harp.
  Refrain

4 Why should I be afraid in evil days, *
  when the wickedness of those at
  my heels surrounds me,

5 The wickedness of those who put their
  trust in their goods, *
  and boast of their great riches? *Refrain*

7 For the ransom of our life is so great, *
  that we should never have
  enough to pay it,

8 In order to live for ever and ever, *
  and never see the grave. *Refrain*

9 For we see that the wise die also;
  like the dull and stupid they perish *
  and leave their wealth to those who
  come after them.

10 Their graves shall be their homes for ever,
  their dwelling places from generation to
  generation, *
  though they call the lands after their own
  names.

11 Even though honored, they cannot live for
  ever; *
  they are like the beasts that perish.
  Refrain

Out of Zi - on, per - fect in its beau - ty, God re - veals him - self in glo - ry.

1   The Lord, the God of gods, has spoken; *
        he has called the earth from the
        rising of the sun to its setting.   *Refrain*

3   Our God will come and will not keep silence; *
        before him there is a consuming flame,
        and round about him a raging storm.
4   He calls the heavens and the earth from above *
        to witness the judgment of his people.
                                        Refrain
5   "Gather before me my loyal followers, *
        those who have made a covenant with
        me and sealed it with sacrifice."
6   Let the heavens declare the rightness
of his cause; *
        for God himself is judge.   *Refrain*

Psalm 51

RCL Psalm 51:1-13   Lent 5B
RCL/BCP Psalm 51:1-11   Proper 19C
BCP Psalm 51:11-16   Lent 5B

(Create in me)

1 Have mercy on me, O God, according to
your loving-kindness; *
    in your great compassion blot
    out my offenses.
2 Wash me through and through from
my wickedness *
    and cleanse me from my sin.   *Refrain*

3 For I know my transgressions, *
    and my sin is ever before me.
4 Against you only have I sinned *
    and done what is evil in your sight.
       Refrain
5 And so you are justified when you speak *
    and upright in your judgment.
6 Indeed, I have been wicked from my birth, *
    a sinner from my mother's womb.
       Refrain
7 For behold, you look for truth deep within me, *
    and will make me understandwisdom
    secretly.
8 Purge me from my sin, and I shall be pure; *
wash me, and I shall be clean indeed.

   Refrain

9 Make me hear of joy and gladness, *
    that the body you have broken may rejoice.
10 Hide your face from my sins *
    and blot out all my iniquities.   *Refrain*

11 Create in me a clean heart, O God, *
    and renew a right spirit within me.
12 Cast me not away from your presence *
    and take not your holy Spirit from me.
13 Give me the joy of your saving help again *
    and sustain me with your bountiful Spirit.
       Refrain
14 I shall teach your ways to the wicked, *
    and sinners shall return to you.
15 Deliver me from death, O God, *
    and my tongue shall sing of your
    righteousness, O God of my salvation.
16 Open my lips, O Lord, *
    and my mouth shall proclaim your praise.
       Refrain

Psalm 51

(Have mercy on me)

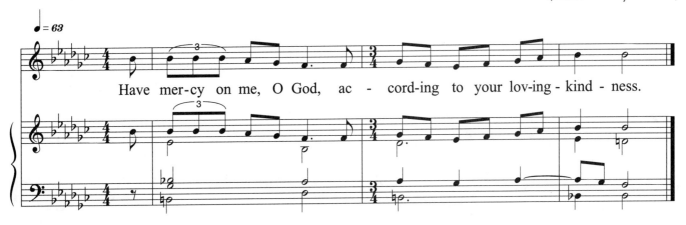

1 Have mercy on me, O God, according to your loving-kindness; *
>> in your great compassion blot out my offenses.

2 Wash me through and through from my wickedness *
>> and cleanse me from my sin.   *Refrain*

3 For I know my transgressions, *
>> and my sin is ever before me.

4 Against you only have I sinned *
>> and done what is evil in your sight.   *Refrain*

5 And so you are justified when you speak *
>> and upright in your judgment.

6 Indeed, I have been wicked from my birth, *
>> a sinner from my mother's womb.   *Refrain*

7 For behold, you look for truth deep within me, *
>> and will make me understandwisdom secretly.

8 Purge me from my sin, and I shall be pure; *
>> wash me, and I shall be clean indeed.   *Refrain*

9 Make me hear of joy and gladness, *
>> that the body you have broken may rejoice.

10 Hide your face from my sins *
>> and blot out all my iniquities.   *Refrain*

11 Create in me a clean heart, O God, *
>> and renew a right spirit within me.

12 Cast me not away from your presence *
>> and take not your holy Spirit from me.

13 Give me the joy of your saving help again *
>> and sustain me with your bountiful Spirit.   *Refrain*

Psalm 54

RCL Psalm 54   Proper 20B
BCP Psalm 54   Proper 20B

God is my help - er; the Lord su - stains my life.

1   Save me, O God, by your Name; *
     in your might, defend my cause.
2   Hear my prayer, O God; *
     give ear to the words of my mouth.
3   For the arrogant have risen up against me,
     and the ruthless have sought my life, *
       those who have no regard for God.

Refrain

4   Behold, God is my helper; *
     it is the Lord who sustains my life.
5   Render evil to those who spy on me; *
     in your faithfulness, destroy them.

Refrain

6   I will offer you a freewill sacrifice *
     and praise your Name, O Lord, for it is good.
7   For you have rescued me from every trouble, *
     and my eye has seen the ruin of my foes.

Refrain

For God a - lone my soul in si - lence waits.

6 For God alone my soul in silence waits; *
    truly, my hope is in him.

7 He alone is my rock and my salvation, *
    my stronghold, so that I shall
    not be shaken.

8 In God is my safety and my honor; *
    God is my strong rock and my refuge.
                         Refrain

9 Put your trust in him always, O people, *
    pour out your hearts before him,
    for God is our refuge.

10 Those of high degree are but a fleeting
  breath, *
    even those of low estate cannot be
    trusted.

11 On the scales they are lighter than a breath, *
    all of them together.   *Refrain*

12 Put no trust in extortion;
  in robbery take no empty pride; *
    though wealth increase, set not
    your heart upon it.

13 God has spoken once, twice have I heard it, *
    that power belongs to God.

14 Steadfast love is yours, O Lord, *
    for you repay everyone according to his
  deeds.   *Refrain*

Psalm 63

BCP Psalm 63:1-8   Proper 7C

Lord, my soul clings to you; your right hand holds me fast.

1   O God, you are my God; eagerly I seek you; *
      my soul thirsts for you, my flesh faints
      for you, as in a barren and dry land
      where there is no water.

2   Therefore I have gazed upon you in
    your holy place, *
      that I might behold your power
      and your glory.   *Refrain*

3   For your loving-kindness is better than life
    itself; *
      my lips shall give you praise.

4   So will I bless you as long as I live *
      and lift up my hands in your Name.
                                   Refrain

5   My soul is content, as with marrow and
    fatness, *
      and my mouth praises you with joyful
      lips,

6   When I remember you upon my bed, *
      and meditate on you in the night
      watches.   *Refrain*

7   For you have been my helper, *
      and under the shadow of your wings
      I will rejoice.

8   My soul clings to you; *
      your right hand holds me fast.   *Refrain*

1 You are to be praised, O God, in Zion; *
        to you shall vows be performed
        in Jerusalem.
2 To you that hear prayer shall all flesh come, *
        because of their transgressions. *Refrain*

3 Our sins are stronger than we are, *
        but you will blot them out.
4 Happy are they whom you choose
   and draw to your courts to dwell there! *
        they will be satisfied by the beauty of
        your house, by the holiness of your
        temple.   *Refrain*

5 Awesome things will you show us in
   your righteousness, O God of our salvation, *
        O Hope of all the ends of the earth
        and of the seas that are far away.
6 You make fast the mountains by your power; *
        they are girded about with might.
                                         Refrain

7 You still the roaring of the seas, *
        the roaring of their waves,
        and the clamor of the peoples.

8 Those who dwell at the ends of the earth will
   tremble at your marvelous signs; *
        you make the dawn and the dusk to
        sing for joy.   *Refrain*

9 You visit the earth and water it abundantly;
   you make it very plenteous; *
        the river of God is full of water.
10 You prepare the grain, *
        for so you provide for the earth.
11 You drench the furrows and smooth out the ridges; *
        with heavy rain you soften the ground
        and bless its increase.   *Refrain*

13 May the fields of the wilderness be rich for grazing, *
        and the hills be clothed with joy.
14 May the meadows cover themselves with flocks,
   and the valleys cloak themselves with grain; *
        let them shout for joy and sing. *Refrain*

Psalm 66

RCL Psalm 66:7-18   Easter 6A
RCL Psalm 66:1-8   Proper 9C
RCL Psalm 66:10-14   Proper 9C
RCL Psalm 66:1-11   Proper 23C

(RCL)

Be joy - ful in God,   all you lands.

1 Be joyful in God, all you lands; *
      sing the glory of his Name;
      sing the glory of his praise.
2 Say to God, "How awesome are your deeds! *
      because of your great strength your
      enemies cringe before you.   *Refrain*

3 All the earth bows down before you, *
      sings to you, sings out your Name."
4 Come now and see the works of God, *
      how wonderful he is in his doing
      toward all people.   *Refrain*

5 He turned the sea into dry land,
      so that they went through the water on foot, *
      and there we rejoiced in him.
6 In his might he rules for ever;
      his eyes keep watch over the nations; *
      let no rebel rise up against him. *Refrain*

7 Bless our God, you peoples; *
      make the voice of his praise to be heard;
8 Who holds our souls in life, *
      and will not allow our feet to slip.
                                    Refrain

Text continues on next page

Be joy-ful in God, all you lands.

9 For you, O God, have proved us; *
   you have tried us just as silver is tried.
10 You brought us into the snare; *
   you laid heavy burdens upon our backs.
11 You let enemies ride over our heads;
   we went through fire and water; *
      but you brought us out into a
      place of refreshment.   *Refrain*

12 I will enter your house with burnt-offerings
   and will pay you my vows, *
      which I promised with my lips and spoke
      with my mouth when I was in trouble.
13 I will offer you sacrifices of fat beasts
   with the smoke of rams; *
      I will give you oxen and goats.   *Refrain*

14 Come and listen, all you who fear God, *
   and I will tell you what he has done for me.
15 I called out to him with my mouth, *
   and his praise was on my tongue. *Refrain*

16 If I had found evil in my heart, *
   the Lord would not have heard me;
17 But in truth God has heard me; *
   he has attended to the voice of my prayer.
18 Blessed be God, who has not rejected my
   prayer, *
      nor withheld his love from me.   *Refrain*

Psalm 67

RCL Psalm 67   Proper 15A, Easter 6C
BCP Psalm 67   Proper 15A, Easter 6C

Let the peo-ples praise you, O God; let all the peo - ples

praise you.

1   May God be merciful to us and bless us, *
      show us the light of his countenance and come to us.
2   Let your ways be known upon earth, *
      your saving health among all nations.
                                          Refrain
4   Let the nations be glad and sing for joy, *
      for you judge the peoples with equity
      and guide all the nations upon earth.
                                          Refrain
6   The earth has brought forth her increase; *
      may God, our own God, give us his blessing.
7   May God give us his blessing, *
      and may all the ends of the earth stand in awe of him.
                                          Refrain

Page has been left blank
to facilitate page turns.

Psalm 68

(RCL)

Sing to God, O king-doms of the earth; sing prais-es to the Lord.

1 Let God arise, and let his enemies be scattered; *
> let those who hate him flee before him.

2 Let them vanish like smoke when the wind drives it away; *
> as the wax melts at the fire, so let the wicked perish at the presence of God.

3 But let the righteous be glad and rejoice before God; *
> let them also be merry and joyful.
>
> *Refrain*

4 Sing to God, sing praises to his Name; exalt him who rides upon the heavens; *
> Yahweh is his Name, rejoice before him!

5 Father of orphans, defender of widows, *
> God in his holy habitation!

6 God gives the solitary a home and brings forth prisoners into freedom; *
> but the rebels shall live in dry places.
>
> *Refrain*

7 O God, when you went forth before your people, *
> when you marched through the wilderness,

8 The earth shook, and the skies poured down rain, at the presence of God, the God of Sinai, *
> at the presence of God, the God of Israel.
>
> *Refrain*

9 You sent a gracious rain, O God, upon your inheritance; *
> you refreshed the land when it was weary.

10 Your people found their home in it; *
> in your goodness, O God, you have made provision for the poor.   *Refrain*

11 The Lord gave the word; *
> great was the company of women who bore the tidings:

12 "Kings with their armies are fleeing away; *
> the women at home are dividing the spoils."
>
> *Refrain*

Text continues on next page

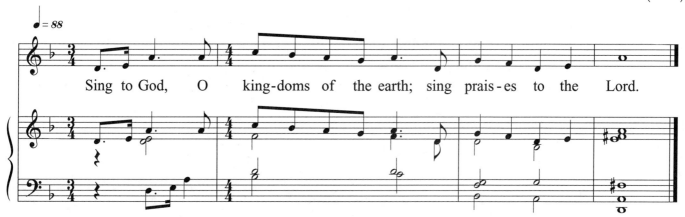

Sing to God, O king-doms of the earth; sing prais-es to the Lord.

13 Though you lingered among the sheepfolds, *
  you shall be like a dove whose wings are
  covered with silver, whose feathers are
  like green gold.

14 When the Almighty scattered kings, *
  it was like snow falling in Zalmon.
                                    Refrain

15 O mighty mountain, O hill of Bashan! *
  O rugged mountain, O hill of Bashan!

16 Why do you look with envy, O rugged
  mountain, at the hill which God chose for
  his resting place? *
    truly, the Lord will dwell there for ever.
                                    Refrain

17 The chariots of God are twenty thousand,
  even thousands of thousands; *
    the Lord comes in holiness from Sinai.

18 You have gone up on high and led
  captivity captive; you have received gifts
  even from your enemies, *
    that the Lord God might dwell among them.
                                    Refrain

19 Blessed be the Lord day by day, *
  the God of our salvation, whobears our
  burdens.

20 He is our God, the God of our salvation; *
  God is the Lord, by whom we escape
  death.   *Refrain*

34 He rides in the heavens, the ancient heavens; *
  he sends forth his voice, his mighty voice.

35 Ascribe power to God; *
  his majesty is over Israel;
  his strength is in the skies.

36 How wonderful is God in his holy places! *
  the God of Israel giving strength and
  power to his people!
  Blessed be God!   *Refrain*

Psalm 72

RCL Psalm 72:1-7, 10-14   The Epiphany ABC
BCP Psalm 72:1-2, 10-17   The Epiphany ABC

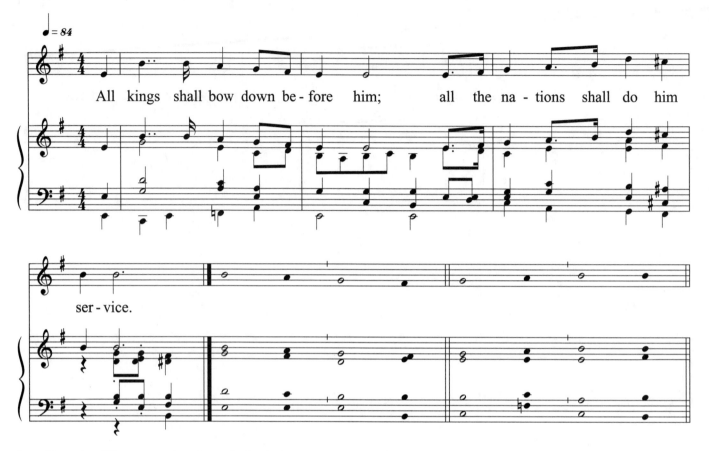

All kings shall bow down be-fore him; all the na-tions shall do him ser-vice.

1 Give the King your justice, O God, *
    and your righteousness to the King's Son;
2 That he may rule your people righteously *
    and the poor with justice;   (Refrain)
3 That the mountains may bring prosperity
   to the people, *
    and the little hills bring righteousness.
4 He shall defend the needy among the
   people; *
    he shall rescue the poor and crush
    the oppressor.   Refrain

5 He shall live as long as the sun and
   moon endure, *
    from one generation to another.
6 He shall come down like rain upon
   the mown field, *
    like showers that water the earth.
7 In his time shall the righteous flourish; *
    there shall be abundance of peace till
    the moon shall be no more.   Refrain

10 The kings of Tarshish and of the isles
    shall pay tribute, *
    and the kings of Arabia and Saba offer gifts.
                                         Refrain
12 For he shall deliver the poor who cries
    out in distress, *
    and the oppressed who has no helper.
13 He shall have pity on the lowly and poor; *
    he shall preserve the lives of the needy.
14 He shall redeem their lives from
    oppression and violence, *
    and dear shall their blood be in his sight.
                                         Refrain
15 Long may he live! and may there be given to
    him gold from Arabia; *
    may prayer be made for him always,
    and may they bless him all the day long.
16 May there be abundance of grain on the earth,
    growing thick even on the hilltops; *
    may its fruit flourish like Lebanon,
    and its grain like grass upon the earth.
17 May his Name remain for ever and be
    established as long as the sun endures; *
    may all the nations bless themselves in
    him and call him blessed.   Refrain

*When singing the RCL, skip the refrain
at verse 2 and continue to verse 4*

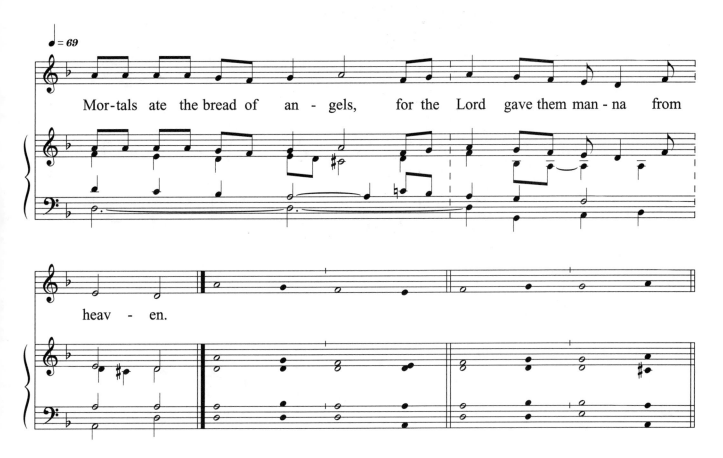

Mor-tals ate the bread of an - gels, for the Lord gave them man - na from heav - en.

14 He led them with a cloud by day, *
    and all the night through with a
    glow of fire.
15 He split the hard rocks in the wilderness *
    and gave them drink as from
    the great deep.
16 He brought streams out of the cliff, *
    and the waters gushed out like rivers.
                                    Refrain
17 But they went on sinning against him, *
    rebelling in the desert against
    the Most High.
18 They tested God in their hearts, *
    demanding food for their craving.
19 They railed against God and said, *
    "Can God set a table in the wilderness?
20 True, he struck the rock, the waters gushed
    out, and the gullies overflowed; *
    but is he able to give bread
    or to provide meat for his people?"
                                    Refrain

23 So he commanded the clouds above *
    and opened the doors of heaven.
24 He rained down manna upon them to eat *
    and gave them grain from heaven.
25 So mortals ate the bread of angels; *
    he provided for them food enough.
                                    Refrain

Psalm 80

RCL Psalm 80:1-7, 16-18   Advent 4A, Advent 1B
RCL Psalm 80:1-7   Advent 4C
BCP Psalm 80:1-7   Advent 1B, Advent 4C

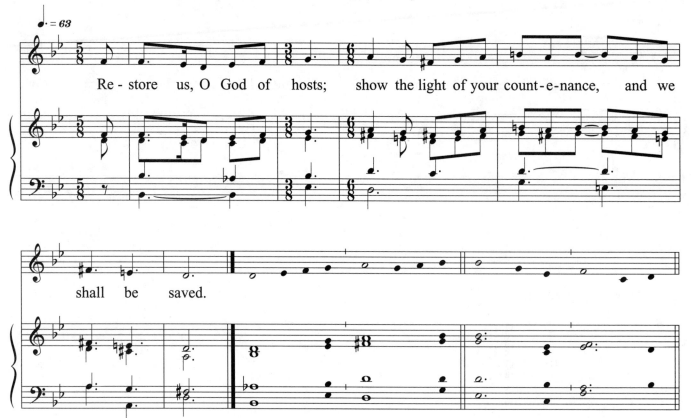

Re - store us, O God of hosts; show the light of your count-e-nance, and we shall be saved.

1   Hear, O Shepherd of Israel, leading Joseph
like a flock; *
> shine forth, you that are enthroned
> upon the cherubim.

2   In the presence of Ephraim, Benjamin,
and Manasseh, *
> stir up your strength and come
> to help us.   *Refrain*

4   O Lord God of hosts, *
> how long will you be angered
> despite the prayers of your people?

5   You have fed them with the bread of tears; *
> you have given them bowls of
> tears to drink.

6   You have made us the derision of
our neighbors, *
> and our enemies laugh us to scorn.
>   *Refrain*

16   Let your hand be upon the man of
your right hand, *
> the son of man you have made so
> strong for yourself.

17   And so will we never turn away from you; *
> give us life, that we may call
> upon your Name.   *Refrain*

1   God takes his stand in the council of heaven; *
      he gives judgment in the midst of the gods:
2   "How long will you judge unjustly, *
      and show favor to the wicked?   *Refrain*

3   Save the weak and the orphan; *
      defend the humble and needy;
4   Rescue the weak and the poor; *
      deliver them from the power of the wicked.
                     Refrain

5   They do not know, neither do they understand;
    they go about in darkness; *
      all the foundations of the earth are shaken.
                     Refrain

6   Now I say to you, 'You are gods, *
      and all of you children of the Most High;
7   Nevertheless, you shall die like mortals, *
      and fall like any prince.'"   *Refrain*

Psalm 84

RCL/BCP Psalm 84:1-8   Christmas 2 ABC
RCL Psalm 84   Proper 16B
RCL/BCP Psalm 84:1-6   Proper 25C

How dear to me is your dwelling, O Lord of hosts!

1   How dear to me is your dwelling,
    O Lord of hosts! *
        My soul has a desire and longing for
        the courts of the Lord; my heart and
        my flesh rejoice in the living God.
                                            Refrain

2   The sparrow has found her a house
    and the swallow a nest where she may
    lay her young; *
        by the side of your altars, O Lord of hosts,
        my King and my God.

3   Happy are they who dwell in your house! *
        they will always be praising you. *Refrain*

4   Happy are the people whose strength is
    in you! *
        whose hearts are set on the pilgrims' way.

5   Those who go through the desolate valley
    will find it a place of springs, *
        for the early rains have covered it with
        pools of water.

6   They will climb from height to height, *
        and the God of gods will reveal
        himself in Zion.   *Refrain*

7   Lord God of hosts, hear my prayer; *
        hearken, O God of Jacob.

8   Behold our defender, O God; *
        and look upon the face of your Anointed.
                                            Refrain

9   For one day in your courts is better than
    a thousand in my own room, *
        and to stand at the threshold of the
        house of my God than to dwell in the
        tents of the wicked.

10 For the Lord God is both sun and shield; *
        he will give grace and glory;

11 No good thing will the Lord withhold *
        from those who walk with integrity.

12 O Lord of hosts, *
        happy are they who put their trust in you!
                                            Refrain

Page has been left blank
to facilitate page turns.

Psalm 85

RCL Psalm 85:8-13 Proper 14A, Proper 10B
RCL Psalm 85:1-2, 8-13 Advent 2B
RCL Psalm 85 Proper 12C

(RCL)

♩ = 88 **may be sung as a 2-part round**

Show us your mer - cy, show us your mer - cy, O Lord.

Show us your mer - cy, show us your mer - cy, and grant us your sal -

va - tion.

1 You have been gracious to your land, O Lord, *
  you have restored the good fortune
  of Jacob.

2 You have forgiven the iniquity of
  your people *
    and blotted out all their sins. *Refrain*

3 You have withdrawn all your fury *
  and turned yourself from your
  wrathful indignation.

4 Restore us then, O God our Savior; *
  let your anger depart from us. *Refrain*

5 Will you be displeased with us for ever? *
  will you prolong your anger from
  age to age?

6 Will you not give us life again, *
  that your people may rejoice in you?
    Refrain

Text continues on next page

Psalm 85

(BCP)

Show us your mer-cy, show us your mer-cy, O Lord.

Show us your mer-cy, show us your mer-cy, and grant us your sal-

va-tion.

8 I will listen to what the Lord God is saying, *
    for he is speaking peace to his
    faithful people and to those who turn
    their hearts to him.
9 Truly, his salvation is very near to those
    who fear him, *
      that his glory may dwell in our land.
                        Refrain

10 Mercy and truth have met together; *
     righteousness and peace have
     kissed each other.
11 Truth shall spring up from the earth, *
     and righteousness shall look
     down from heaven.   *Refrain*

12 The Lord will indeed grant prosperity, *
     and our land will yield its increase.
13 Righteousness shall go before him, *
     and peace shall be a pathway for his feet.
                        Refrain

Psalm 89

RCL Psalm 89:1-29   Epiphany 1 ABC
RCL Psalm 89:19-37   Proper 11B
BCP Psalm 89:1-29   Epiphany 1 ABC
BCP Psalm 89:19-29   Epiphany 1 ABC

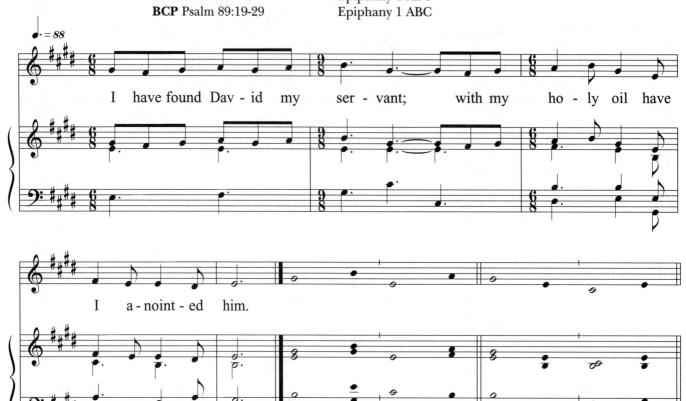

I have found Dav - id my ser - vant; with my ho - ly oil have

I a - noint - ed him.

1 Your love, O Lord, for ever will I sing; *
    from age to age my mouth will
    proclaim your faithfulness.

2 For I am persuaded that your love is
established for ever; *
    you have set your faithfulness firmly
    in the heavens.   *Refrain*

3 "I have made a covenant with my
chosen one; *
    I have sworn an oath to David my servant:

4 'I will establish your line for ever, *
    and preserve your throne for all
    generations.'"   *Refrain*

5 The heavens bear witness to your wonders,
O Lord, *
    and to your faithfulness in the assembly
    of the holy ones;

6 For who in the skies can be compared
to the Lord? *
who is like the Lord among the gods?

7 God is much to be feared in the council of
the holy ones, *
    great and terrible to all those round
    about him.

8 Who is like you, Lord God of hosts? *
    O mighty Lord, your faithfulness is all
    around you.   *Refrain*

9 You rule the raging of the sea *
    and still the surging of its waves.

10 You have crushed Rahab of the deep with
a deadly wound; *
    you have scattered your enemies with
    your mighty arm.   *Refrain*

11 Yours are the heavens; the earth also is yours; *
    you laid the foundations of the world and
    all that is in it.

12 You have made the north and the south; *
    Tabor and Hermon rejoice in your Name.
               Refrain

Text continues on next page

13 You have a mighty arm; *
    strong is your hand and high is your
    right hand.
14 Righteousness and justice are the foundations
of your throne; *
    love and truth go before your face.
                                 Refrain
15 Happy are the people who know the festal shout! *
    they walk, O Lord, in the light of your
    presence.
16 They rejoice daily in your Name; *
    they are jubilant in your righteousness.
17 For you are the glory of their strength, *
    and by your favor our might is exalted.
18 Truly, the Lord is our ruler; *
    the Holy One of Israel is our King.
                                 Refrain
19 You spoke once in a vision and said to
your faithful people: *
    "I have set the crown upon a warrior
    and have exalted one chosen out of
    the people.
20 I have found David my servant; *
    with my holy oil have I anointed him.
21 My hand will hold him fast *
    and my arm will make him strong.
                                 Refrain
22 No enemy shall deceive him, *
    nor any wicked man bring him down.
23 I will crush his foes before him *
    and strike down those who hate him.
                                 Refrain

24 My faithfulness and love shall be with him, *
    and he shall be victorious through
    my Name.
25 I shall make his dominion extend *
    from the Great Sea to the River. *Refrain*

26 He will say to me, 'You are my Father, *
    my God, and the rock of my salvation.'
27 I will make him my firstborn *
    and higher than the kings of the earth.
                                 Refrain
28 I will keep my love for him for ever, *
    and my covenant will stand firm for him.
29 I will establish his line for ever *
    and his throne as the days of heaven."
                                 Refrain
30 "If his children forsake my law *
    and do not walk according to my
    judgments;
31 If they break my statutes *
    and do not keep my commandments;
32 I will punish their transgressions with a rod *
    and their iniquities with the lash;
33 But I will not take my love from him, *
    nor let my faithfulness prove false.
                                 Refrain
34 I will not break my covenant, *
    nor change what has gone out of my lips.
35 Once for all I have sworn by my holiness: *
    'I will not lie to David. *Refrain*

36 His line shall endure for ever *
    and his throne as the sun before me;
37 It shall stand fast for evermore like the moon, *
    the abiding witness in the sky.'" *Refrain*

Psalm 90

RCL Psalm 90:1-8, (9-11), 12   Proper 28A
BCP Psalm 90:1-8, 12   Proper 28A, Proper 23B

(vss. 1-8, 9-11, 12)

Teach us to num-ber our days that we may ap-ply our hearts to wis - dom.

1   Lord, you have been our refuge *
        from one generation to another.
2   Before the mountains were brought forth,
    or the land and the earth were born, *
        from age to age you are God.   *Refrain*

3   You turn us back to the dust and say, *
        "Go back, O child of earth."
4   For a thousand years in your sight are like
    yesterday when it is past *
        and like a watch in the night.   *Refrain*

5   You sweep us away like a dream; *
        we fade away suddenly like the grass.
6   In the morning it is green and flourishes; *
        in the evening it is dried up and
        withered.   *Refrain*

7   For we consume away in your displeasure; *
        we are afraid because of your
        wrathful indignation.
8   Our iniquities you have set before you, *
        and our secret sins in the light of
        your countenance.   *Refrain*

9   When you are angry, all our days are gone; *
        we bring our years to an end like a sigh.
10 The span of our life is seventy years,
    perhaps in strength even eighty; *
        yet the sum of them is but labor and sorrow,
        for they pass away quickly and we are gone.
                                                    Refrain
11 Who regards the power of your wrath? *
        who rightly fears your indignation?
                                                    Refrain

13 Return, O Lord; how long will you tarry? *
        be gracious to your servants.
14 Satisfy us by your loving-kindness in the morning; *
        so shall we rejoice and be glad all the days of our life.
15 Make us glad by the measure of the days that you afflicted us *
        and the years in which we suffered adversity.

Refrain

16 Show your servants your works *
        and your splendor to their children.
17 May the graciousness of the Lord our God be upon us; *
        prosper the work of our hands; prosper our handiwork.

Refrain

Psalm 91

RCL Psalm 91:9-16   Proper 24B
RCL Psalm 91:1-6, 14-16   Proper 21C
BCP Psalm 91:9-16   Proper 24B

Be-cause he is bound to me in love, there-fore will I de-liv-er him.

1 He who dwells in the shelter of
the Most High, *
    abides under the shadow of
    the Almighty.
2 He shall say to the Lord,
"You are my refuge and my stronghold, *
    my God in whom I put my trust." *Refrain*

3 He shall deliver you from the snare
of the hunter *
    and from the deadly pestilence.
4 He shall cover you with his pinions,
and you shall find refuge under his wings; *
    his faithfulness shall be a shield
    and buckler. *Refrain*

5 You shall not be afraid of any terror by night, *
    nor of the arrow that flies by day;
6 Of the plague that stalks in the darkness, *
    nor of the sickness that lays waste at mid-day.
                              Refrain

9 Because you have made the Lord your refuge, *
    and the Most High your habitation,
10 There shall no evil happen to you, *
    neither shall any plague come near
    your dwelling.   *Refrain*

11 For he shall give his angels charge over you, *
    to keep you in all your ways.
12 They shall bear you in their hands, *
    lest you dash your foot against a stone.
13 You shall tread upon the lion and adder; *
    you shall trample the young lion
    and the serpent under your feet.
                              Refrain
14 Because he is bound to me in love,
    therefore will I deliver him; *
        I will protect him, because he knows
        my Name.
15 He shall call upon me, and I will answer him; *
        I am with him in trouble;
        I will rescue him and bring him to honor.
16 With long life will I satisfy him, *
        and show him my salvation.   *Refrain*

The Lord shall reign for ev-er and ev-er. The Lord shall reign for ev-er.

1   The Lord is King;
    he has put on splendid apparel; *
        the Lord has put on his apparel
        and girded himself with strength.
2   He has made the whole world so sure *
        that it cannot be moved;
3   Ever since the world began, your throne
    has been established; *
        you are from everlasting.   *Refrain*

4   The waters have lifted up, O Lord,
    the waters have lifted up their voice; *
        the waters have lifted up their pounding waves.
5   Mightier than the sound of many waters,
    mightier than the breakers of the sea, *
        mightier is the Lord who dwells on high.
6   Your testimonies are very sure, *
        and holiness adorns your house, O Lord,
        for ever and for evermore.   *Refrain*

Psalm 95

To-day if you would hear his voice, hard-en not your hearts.

1   Come, let us sing to the Lord; *
      let us shout for joy to the Rock of
      our salvation.

2   Let us come before his presence
   with thanksgiving *
      and raise a loud shout to him with psalms.

3   For the Lord is a great God, *
      and a great King above all gods. *Refrain*

4   In his hand are the caverns of the earth, *
      and the heights of the hills are his also.

5   The sea is his, for he made it, *
      and his hands have molded the dry land.
                         Refrain

6   Come, let us bow down, and bend the knee, *
      and kneel before the Lord our Maker.

7   For he is our God, and we are the people
   of his pasture and the sheep of his hand. *
      Oh, that today you would hearken
      to his voice!   *Refrain*

8   Harden not your hearts,
   as your forebears did in the wilderness, *
      at Meribah, and on that day at Massah,
      when they tempted me.

9   They put me to the test, *
      though they had seen my works. *Refrain*

10 Forty years long I detested that
   generation and said, *
      "This people are wayward in their hearts;
      they do not know my ways."

11 So I swore in my wrath, *
      "They shall not enter into my rest."
                         Refrain

RCL Psalm 96   Christmas Day 1 ABC
BCP Psalm 96:1-4, 11-12   Christmas Day 1 ABC

To-day is born our Sa - vior, Christ the Lord.

1   Sing to the Lord a new song; *
        sing to the Lord, all the whole earth.
2   Sing to the Lord and bless his Name; *
        proclaim the good news of his salvation
        from day to day.   *Refrain*

3   Declare his glory among the nations *
        and his wonders among all peoples.
4   For great is the Lord and greatly to be praised; *
        he is more to be feared than all gods.
                                            Refrain

5   As for all the gods of the nations, they
    are but idols; *
        but it is the Lord who made the heavens.
6   Oh, the majesty and magnificence of
    his presence! *
        Oh, the power and the splendor of
        his sanctuary!   *Refrain*

7   Ascribe to the Lord, you families of the peoples; *
        ascribe to the Lord honor and power.
8   Ascribe to the Lord the honor due his Name; *
        bring offerings and come into his courts.
                                            Refrain
9   Worship the Lord in the beauty of holiness; *
        let the whole earth tremble before him.
10 Tell it out among the nations: "The Lord is King! *
        he has made the world so firm that it
        cannot be moved; he will judge the
        peoples with equity."
                                            Refrain
11 Let the heavens rejoice, and let the earth be glad;
    let the sea thunder and all that is in it; *
        let the field be joyful and all that is therein.
12 Then shall all the trees of the wood shout for joy
    before the Lord when he comes, *
        when he comes to judge the earth.
                                            Refrain
13 He will judge the world with righteousness *
        and the peoples with his truth.   *Refrain*

Psalm 98

RCL Psalm 98　　　　Christmas Day 3 ABC
BCP Psalm 98:1-6　　Christmas Day 3 ABC

(All the ends of the earth)

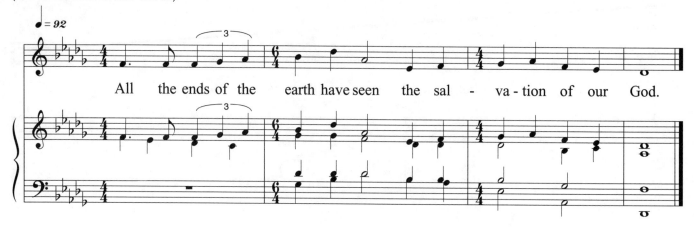

All the ends of the earth have seen the sal - va - tion of our God.

1　Sing to the Lord a new song, *
　　　for he has done marvelous things.
2　With his right hand and his holy arm *
　　　has he won for himself the victory.
　　　　　　　　　　　　　　　　Refrain
3　The Lord has made known his victory; *
　　　his righteousness has he openly shown
　　　in the sight of the nations.
4　He remembers his mercy and faithfulness
　　to the house of Israel, *
　　　and all the ends of the earth have seen
　　　the victory of our God. 　　*Refrain*

5　Shout with joy to the Lord, all you lands; *
　　　lift up your voice, rejoice, and sing.
6　Sing to the Lord with the harp, *
　　　with the harp and the voice of song.
7　With trumpets and the sound of the horn *
　　　shout with joy before the King, the Lord.
　　　　　　　　　　　　　　　　Refrain

8　Let the sea make a noise and all that is in it, *
　　　the lands and those who dwell therein.
9　Let the rivers clap their hands, *
　　　and let the hills ring out with joy before
　　　the Lord, when he comes to judge the earth.
10　In righteousness shall he judge the world *
　　　and the peoples with equity. 　*Refrain*

1 Sing to the Lord a new song, *
      for he has done marvelous things.
2 With his right hand and his holy arm *
      has he won for himself the victory.
                                    Refrain
3 The Lord has made known his victory; *
      his righteousness has he openly shown
      in the sight of the nations.
4 He remembers his mercy and faithfulness
   to the house of Israel, *
      and all the ends of the earth have seen
      the victory of our God.   *Refrain*

5 Shout with joy to the Lord, all you lands; *
      lift up your voice, rejoice, and sing.
6 Sing to the Lord with the harp, *
      with the harp and the voice of song.
7 With trumpets and the sound of the horn *
      shout with joy before the King, the Lord.
                                    Refrain

8 Let the sea make a noise and all that is in it, *
      the lands and those who dwell therein.
9 Let the rivers clap their hands, *
      and let the hills ring out with joy before
      the Lord, when he comes to judge the earth.
10 In righteousness shall he judge the world *
      and the peoples with equity.   *Refrain*

Psalm 99

RCL Psalm 99
BCP Psalm 99

Epiphany Last AC, Proper 24A
Epiphany Last AC

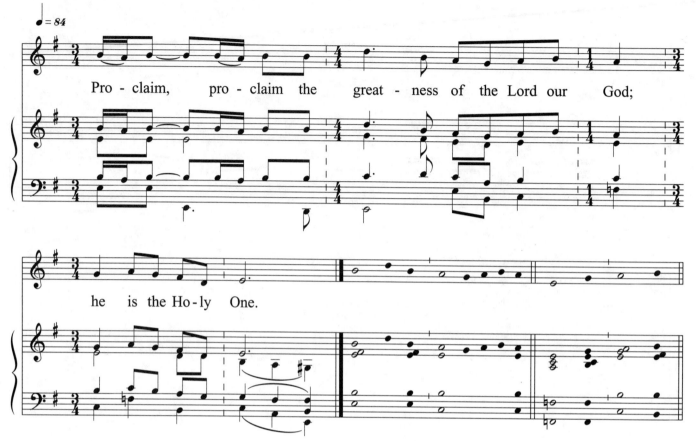

Pro-claim, pro-claim the great-ness of the Lord our God;

he is the Ho-ly One.

1 The Lord is King;
   let the people tremble; *
      he is enthroned upon the cherubim;
      let the earth shake.
2 The Lord is great in Zion; *
      he is high above all peoples.
3 Let them confess his Name, which is
   great and awesome; *
      he is the Holy One. *Refrain*

4 "O mighty King, lover of justice,
   you have established equity; *
      you have executed justice and
      righteousness in Jacob."
5 Proclaim the greatness of the Lord our God
   and fall down before his footstool; *
      he is the Holy One. *Refrain*

6 Moses and Aaron among his priests,
   and Samuel among those who call
   upon his Name, *
      they called upon the Lord, and
      he answered them.
7 He spoke to them out of the pillar of cloud; *
      they kept his testimonies and the decree
      that he gave them. *Refrain*

8 "O Lord our God, you answered them indeed; *
   you were a God who forgave them,
      yet punished them for their evil deeds."
9 Proclaim the greatness of the Lord our God
   and worship him upon his holy hill; *
      for the Lord our God is the Holy One. *Refrain*

1   Be joyful in the Lord, all you lands; *
        serve the Lord with gladness
        and come before his presence with a song.

2   Know this: The Lord himself is God; *
        he himself has made us, and we are his;
        we are his people and the sheep of his pasture.

Refrain

3   Enter his gates with thanksgiving;
    go into his courts with praise; *
        give thanks to him and call upon his Name.

4   For the Lord is good; his mercy is everlasting; *
        and his faithfulness endures from age to age.

Refrain

Psalm 103

RCL Psalm 103:(1-7), 8-13
RCL Psalm 103:1-13, 22

RCL Psalm 103:1-8

Proper 19A
Epiphany 8B,
Proper 3B
Proper 16C

BCP Psalm 103:(1-7), 8-13

BCP Psalm 103:1-6

BCP Psalm 103:1-11

Proper 19A
Epiphany 8B
Proper 3B
Lent 3C

(The Lord is full)

The Lord is full of com-pas-sion and mer-cy, slow to an-ger and of great kind-ness.

1 Bless the Lord, O my soul, *
    and all that is within me,
    bless his holy Name.
2 Bless the Lord, O my soul, *
    and forget not all his benefits.   *Refrain*

3 He forgives all your sins *
    and heals all your infirmities;
4 He redeems your life from the grave *
    and crowns you with mercy and
    loving-kindness;
5 He satisfies you with good things, *
    and your youth is renewed like an
    eagle's.   *Refrain*

6 The Lord executes righteousness *
    and judgment for all who are oppressed.
7 He made his ways known to Moses *
    and his works to the children of Israel.
        Refrain

9 He will not always accuse us, *
    nor will he keep his anger for ever.
10 He has not dealt with us according to our sins, *
    nor rewarded us according to
    our wickedness.   *Refrain*

11 For as the heavens are high above the earth, *
    so is his mercy great upon those
    who fear him.
12 As far as the east is from the west, *
    so far has he removed our sins from us.
13 As a father cares for his children, *
    so does the Lord care for those
    who fear him.   *Refrain*

22 Bless the Lord, all you works of his,
    in all places of his dominion; *
    bless the Lord, O my soul.
        Refrain

70

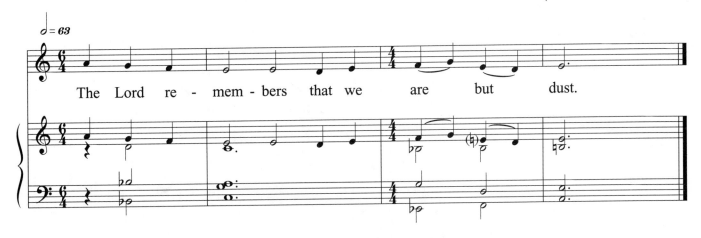

9   He will not always accuse us, *
        nor will he keep his anger for ever.

10 He has not dealt with us according to our sins, *
        nor rewarded us according to our wickedness.

Refrain

11 For as the heavens are high above the earth, *
        so is his mercy great upon those who fear him.

12 As far as the east is from the west, *
        so far has he removed our sins from us.

Refrain

13 As a father cares for his children, *
        so does the Lord care for those who fear him.

14 For he himself knows whereof we are made; *
        he remembers that we are but dust.

Refrain

Psalm 104

RCL Psalm 104:25-35, 37   Vigil of Pentecost ABC, Day of Pentecost ABC
BCP Psalm 104:25-32   Vigil of Pentecost ABC
BCP Psalm 104:25-37   Day of Pentecost ABC

Send forth your Spi - rit, O Lord, and re - new the face of the earth.

25 O Lord, how manifold are your works! *
   in wisdom you have made them all;
      the earth is full of your creatures.

26 Yonder is the great and wide sea
   with its living things too many to number, *
      creatures both small and great.

27 There move the ships,
   and there is that Leviathan, *
      which you have made for the sport of it.
                                    Refrain

28 All of them look to you *
   to give them their food in due season.

29 You give it to them; they gather it; *
   you open your hand, and they are
      filled with good things.   *Refrain*

30 You hide your face, and they are terrified; *
   you take away their breath,
      and they die and return to their dust.

31 You send forth your Spirit, and they
   are created; *
      and so you renew the face of the earth.
                                   Refrain

32 May the glory of the Lord endure for ever; *
   may the Lord rejoice in all his works.
                              (Refrain)

33 He looks at the earth and it trembles; *
   he touches the mountains and they smoke.
                                 Refrain

34 I will sing to the Lord as long as I live; *
   I will praise my God while I have my being.

35 May these words of mine please him; *
   I will rejoice in the Lord.   *Refrain*

> *If ending at verse 32, use refrain in parens. If ending at verse 35 or 37, skip refrain at verse 32.*

36 Let sinners be consumed out of the earth, *
   and the wicked be no more.

37 Bless the Lord, O my soul. *
   Hallelujah!   *Refrain*

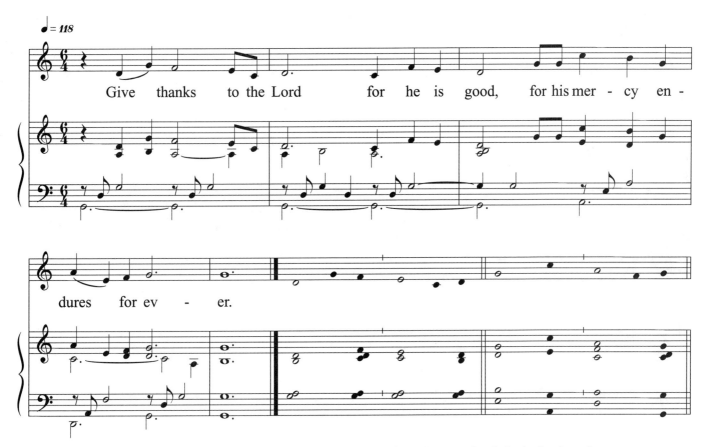

♩ = 118

Give thanks to the Lord   for he is good,   for his mer - cy en -

dures for ev - er.

1   Hallelujah!
    Give thanks to the Lord, for he is good, *
        for his mercy endures for ever.
2   Who can declare the mighty acts of the Lord *
        or show forth all his praise?
3   Happy are those who act with justice *
        and always do what is right!   *Refrain*

4   Remember me, O Lord, with the favor you
    have for your people, *
        and visit me with your saving help;
5   That I may see the prosperity of your elect
    and be glad with the gladness of your people, *
        that I may glory with your inheritance.
                                          Refrain
6   We have sinned as our forebears did; *
        we have done wrong and dealt wickedly.
19 Israel made a bull-calf at Horeb *
        and worshiped a molten image;
20 And so they exchanged their Glory *
        for the image of an ox that feeds on
        grass.   *Refrain*

21 They forgot God their Savior, *
        who had done great things in Egypt,
22 Wonderful deeds in the land of Ham, *
        and fearful things at the Red Sea.
23 So he would have destroyed them,
    had not Moses his chosen stood before him
    in the breach, *
        to turn away his wrath from consuming
        them.   *Refrain*

Psalm 107

RCL Psalm 107:1-7, 33-37   Proper 26A
RCL Psalm 107:1-3, 17-22   Lent 4B
RCL Psalm 107:1-3, 23-32   Proper 7B

Give thanks to the Lord for he is good, and his mer - cy en - dures for ev - er.

2 Let all those whom the Lord has
redeemed proclaim *
     that he redeemed them from the
     hand of the foe.

3 He gathered them out of the lands; *
     from the east and from the west,
     from the north and from the south.
                 Refrain

4 Some wandered in desert wastes; *
     they found no way to a city where
     they might dwell.

5 They were hungry and thirsty; *
     their spirits languished within them.
                 Refrain

6 Then they cried to the Lord in their trouble, *
     and he delivered them from their distress.

7 He put their feet on a straight path *
     to go to a city where they might dwell.
                 Refrain

8 Let them give thanks to the Lord
for his mercy *
     and the wonders he does for his children.

9 For he satisfies the thirsty *
     and fills the hungry with good things.
                 Refrain

10 Some sat in darkness and deep gloom, *
     bound fast in misery and iron;

11 Because they rebelled against the words of God *
     and despised the counsel of the Most High.

12 So he humbled their spirits with hard labor; *
     they stumbled, and there was none to help.
                 Refrain

13 Then they cried to the Lord in their trouble, *
     and he delivered them from their distress.

14 He led them out of darkness and deep gloom *
     and broke their bonds asunder. *Refrain*

Text continues on next page

15 Let them give thanks to the Lord for his mercy *
   and the wonders he does for his children.
16 For he shatters the doors of bronze *
   and breaks in two the iron bars. *Refrain*

17 Some were fools and took to rebellious ways; *
   they were afflicted because of their sins.
18 They abhorred all manner of food *
   and drew near to death's door. *Refrain*

19 Then they cried to the Lord in their trouble, *
   and he delivered them from their distress.
20 He sent forth his word and healed them *
   and saved them from the grave. *Refrain*

21 Let them give thanks to the Lord for his mercy *
   and the wonders he does for his children.
22 Let them offer a sacrifice of thanksgiving *
   and tell of his acts with shouts of joy.
                                          Refrain
23 Some went down to the sea in ships *
   and plied their trade in deep waters;
24 They beheld the works of the Lord *
   and his wonders in the deep. *Refrain*

25 Then he spoke, and a stormy wind arose, *
   which tossed high the waves of the sea.
26 They mounted up to the heavens and fell
   back to the depths; *
   their hearts melted because of their peril.
27 They reeled and staggered like drunkards *
   and were at their wits' end. *Refrain*

28 Then they cried to the Lord in their trouble, *
   and he delivered them from their distress.
29 He stilled the storm to a whisper *
   and quieted the waves of the sea.
30 Then were they glad because of the calm, *
   and he brought them to the harbor they
   were bound for.   *Refrain*

31 Let them give thanks to the Lord for his mercy *
   and the wonders he does for his children.
32 Let them exalt him in the congregation
   of the people *
   and praise him in the council of the elders.
                                          Refrain
33 The Lord changed rivers into deserts, *
   and water-springs into thirsty ground,
34 A fruitful land into salt flats, *
   because of the wickedness of those
   who dwell there.   *Refrain*

35 He changed deserts into pools of water *
   and dry land into water-springs.
36 He settled the hungry there, *
   and they founded a city to dwell in.
37 They sowed fields, and planted vineyards, *
   and brought in a fruitful harvest.
                                          Refrain
43 Whoever is wise will ponder these things, *
   and consider well the mercies of the Lord.
                                          Refrain

Psalm 111

BCP Psalm 111   Easter 2 ABC

The Lord has sent re-demp-tion to his peo - ple, hal - le - lu - jah.

1   Hallelujah!
    I will give thanks to the Lord with my
    whole heart, *
        in the assembly of the upright,
        in the congregation.
2   Great are the deeds of the Lord! *
        they are studied by all who
        delight in them.   *Refrain*

3   His work is full of majesty and splendor, *
        and his righteousness endures for ever.
4   He makes his marvelous works to
    be remembered; *
        the Lord is gracious and full of
        compassion.   *Refrain*

5   He gives food to those who fear him; *
        he is ever mindful of his covenant.
6   He has shown his people the power of his
    works *
        in giving them the lands of the nations.
                                            Refrain
7   The works of his hands are faithfulness
    and justice; *
        all his commandments are sure.
8   They stand fast for ever and ever, *
        because they are done in truth and equity.
9   He sent redemption to his people;
    he commanded his covenant for ever; *
        holy and awesome is his Name.   *Refrain*

10 The fear of the Lord is the beginning of
    wisdom; *
        those who act accordingly have a
        good understanding; his praise endures
        for ever.   *Refrain*

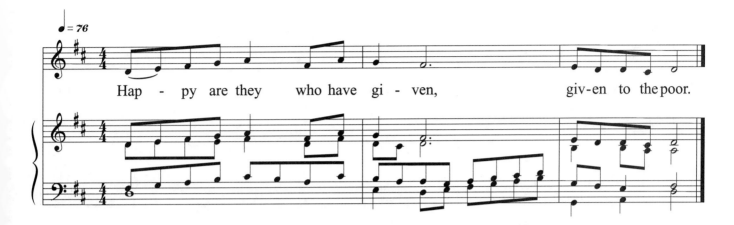

1   Hallelujah!
    Happy are they who fear the Lord *
        and have great delight in
        his commandments!
2   Their descendants will be mighty in the land; *
        the generation of the upright
        will be blessed.
3   Wealth and riches will be in their house, *
        and their righteousness will last for ever.
                                        Refrain
4   Light shines in the darkness for the upright; *
        the righteous are merciful and
        full of compassion.
5   It is good for them to be generous in lending *
        and to manage their affairs with justice.
6   For they will never be shaken; *
        the righteous will be kept in everlasting
        remembrance.   *Refrain*

7   They will not be afraid of any evil rumors; *
        their heart is right;
        they put their trust in the Lord.
8   Their heart is established and will not shrink, *
        until they see their desire
        upon their enemies.   *Refrain*

9   They have given freely to the poor, *
        and their righteousness stands fast for ever;
        they will hold up their head with honor.
10 The wicked will see it and be angry;
        they will gnash their teeth and pine away; *
        the desires of the wicked will perish.
                                        Refrain

Psalm 114

RCL Psalm 114   Easter Vigil: Eucharist ABC, Easter Day: Evening ABC
BCP Psalm 114   Easter Vigil: Eucharist ABC

Hal - le - lu - jah, hal - le - lu - jah, hal - le - lu - jah!

1   Hallelujah!
    When Israel came out of Egypt, *
        the house of Jacob from a people
        of strange speech,

2   Judah became God's sanctuary *
        and Israel his dominion.   *Refrain*

3   The sea beheld it and fled; *
        Jordan turned and went back.

4   The mountains skipped like rams, *
        and the little hills like young sheep.
                             Refrain

5   What ailed you, O sea, that you fled? *
        O Jordan, that you turned back?

6   You mountains, that you skipped like rams? *
        you little hills like young sheep? *Refrain*

7   Tremble, O earth, at the presence of the Lord, *
        at the presence of the God of Jacob,

8   Who turned the hard rock into a pool of water *
        and flint-stone into a flowing spring.
                             Refrain

Page has been left blank
to facilitate page turns.

Psalm 116

RCL Psalm 116:1, 10-17

Maundy Thursday ABC

(I will lift up the cup)

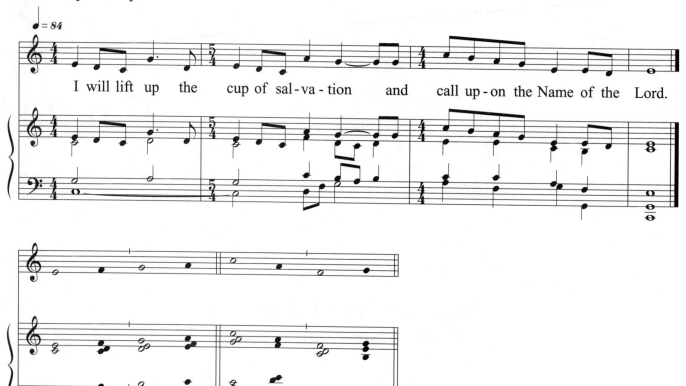

I will lift up the cup of sal-va-tion and call up-on the Name of the Lord.

1   I love the Lord, because he has heard the
voice of my supplication, *
        because he has inclined his ear to me
        whenever I called upon him.
10 How shall I repay the Lord *
        for all the good things he has done for me?
                                        Refrain
12 I will fulfill my vows to the Lord *
        in the presence of all his people.
13 Precious in the sight of the Lord *
        is the death of his servants.   *Refrain*

14 O Lord, I am your servant; *
        I am your servant and the child of your
        handmaid; you have freed me from my
        bonds.
15 I will offer you the sacrifice of thanksgiving *
        and call upon the Name of the Lord.
                                        Refrain
16 I will fulfill my vows to the Lord *
        in the presence of all his people,
17 In the courts of the Lord's house, *
        in the midst of you, O Jerusalem.
        Hallelujah!   *Refrain*

Psalm 116

(I will walk in the presence)

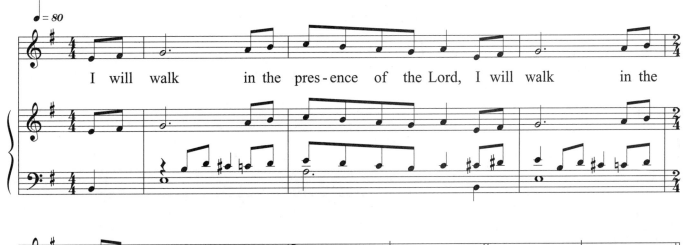

I will walk in the pres-ence of the Lord, I will walk in the

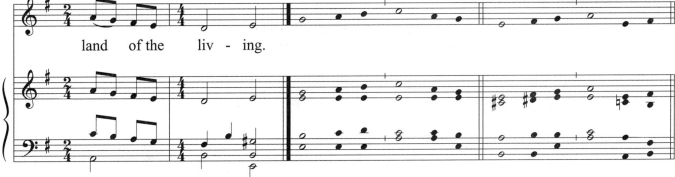

land of the liv-ing.

1 I love the Lord, because he has heard the
voice of my supplication, *
>   because he has inclined his ear to me
>   whenever I called upon him.   *Refrain*

2 The cords of death entangled me;
the grip of the grave took hold of me; *
>   I came to grief and sorrow.

3 Then I called upon the Name of the Lord: *
>   "O Lord, I pray you, save my life."
>   *Refrain*

4 Gracious is the Lord and righteous; *
>   our God is full of compassion.

5 The Lord watches over the innocent; *
>   I was brought very low, and he helped me.
>   *Refrain*

6 Turn again to your rest, O my soul, *
>   for the Lord has treated you well.

7 For you have rescued my life from death, *
>   my eyes from tears, and my feet
>   from stumbling.   *Refrain*

10 How shall I repay the Lord *
>   for all the good things he has done for me?

11 I will lift up the cup of salvation *
>   and call upon the Name of the Lord.
>   *Refrain*

12 I will fulfill my vows to the Lord *
>   in the presence of all his people.

13 Precious in the sight of the Lord *
>   is the death of his servants.   *Refrain*

14 O Lord, I am your servant; *
>   I am your servant and the child of your
>   handmaid; you have freed me from my
>   bonds.

15 I will offer you the sacrifice of thanksgiving *
>   and call upon the Name of the Lord.
>   *Refrain*

16 I will fulfill my vows to the Lord *
>   in the presence of all his people,

17 In the courts of the Lord's house, *
>   in the midst of you, O Jerusalem.
>   Hallelujah!   *Refrain*

Psalm 118

BCP Psalm 118:19-24   Easter 2 ABC

(Give thanks to the Lord)

Give thanks to the Lord for he is good; his mer-cy en-dures for ev - er.

For Easter 2 ABC

19 Open for me the gates of righteousness; *
  I will enter them;
  I will offer thanks to the Lord.

20 "This is the gate of the Lord; *
  he who is righteous may enter." *Refrain*

21 I will give thanks to you, for you answered me *
  and have become my salvation.

22 The same stone which the builders rejected *
  has become the chief cornerstone.

23 This is the Lord's doing, *
  and it is marvelous in our eyes. *Refrain*

24 On this day the Lord has acted; *
  we will rejoice and be glad in it.
        Refrain

For Easter Day ABC

1 Give thanks to the Lord, for he is good; *
  his mercy endures for ever.

2 Let Israel now proclaim, *
  "His mercy endures for ever."

3 Let the house of Aaron now proclaim, *
  "His mercy endures for ever."

4 Let those who fear the Lord now proclaim, *
  "His mercy endures for ever." *Refrain*

5 I called to the Lord in my distress; *
  the Lord answered by setting me free.

6 The Lord is at my side, therefore I will not fear; *
  what can anyone do to me?

7 The Lord is at my side to help me; *
  I will triumph over those who hate me.
        Refrain

8 It is better to rely on the Lord *
  than to put any trust in flesh.

9 It is better to rely on the Lord *
  than to put any trust in rulers. *Refrain*

10 All the ungodly encompass me; *
  in the name of the Lord I will repel them.

11 They hem me in, they hem me in
 on every side; *
  in the name of the Lord I will repel them.
        Refrain

Text continues on next page

12 They swarm about me like bees;
    they blaze like a fire of thorns; *
        in the name of the Lord I will repel them.

13 I was pressed so hard that I almost fell, *
        but the Lord came to my help.   *Refrain*

14 The Lord is my strength and my song, *
        and he has become my salvation.

15 There is a sound of exultation and victory *
        in the tents of the righteous:

16 "The right hand of the Lord has triumphed! *
        the right hand of the Lord is exalted!
        the right hand of the Lord has triumphed!"
                                        Refrain

17 I shall not die, but live, *
        and declare the works of the Lord.

18 The Lord has punished me sorely, *
        but he did not hand me over to death.
                                        Refrain

19 Open for me the gates of righteousness; *
        I will enter them;
        I will offer thanks to the Lord.

20 "This is the gate of the Lord; *
        he who is righteous may enter." *Refrain*

21 I will give thanks to you, for you answered me *
        and have become my salvation.

22 The same stone which the builders rejected *
        has become the chief cornerstone.

23 This is the Lord's doing, *
        and it is marvelous in our eyes. *Refrain*

24 On this day the Lord has acted; *
        we will rejoice and be glad in it.

25 Hosannah, Lord, hosannah! *
        Lord, send us now success.   *Refrain*

26 Blessed is he who comes in the name
    of the Lord; *
        we bless you from the house of the Lord.

27 God is the Lord; he has shined upon us; *
        form a procession with branches up to
        the horns of the altar.

28 "You are my God, and I will thank you; *
        you are my God, and I will exalt you."
                                        Refrain

29 Give thanks to the Lord, for he is good; *
        his mercy endures for ever.   *Refrain*

Psalm 119

RCL Psalm 119:1-8   Epiphany 6A, Proper 1A
RCL Psalm 119:9-16   Lent 5B

(RCL)

Hap - py are they, hap - py are they who walk in the law, the law of the Lord.

1 Happy are they whose way is blameless, *
      who walk in the law of the Lord!
2 Happy are they who observe his decrees *
      and seek him with all their hearts!
                                    Refrain
3 Who never do any wrong, *
      but always walk in his ways.
4 You laid down your commandments, *
      that we should fully keep them. *Refrain*

5 Oh, that my ways were made so direct *
      that I might keep your statutes!
6 Then I should not be put to shame, *
      when I regard all your commandments.
                                    Refrain
7 I will thank you with an unfeigned heart, *
      when I have learned your
      righteous judgments.
8 I will keep your statutes; *
      do not utterly forsake me. *Refrain*

9 How shall a young man cleanse his way? *
      By keeping to your words.
10 With my whole heart I seek you; *
      let me not stray from your commandments.
                                    Refrain
11 I treasure your promise in my heart, *
      that I may not sin against you.
12 Blessed are you, O Lord; *
      instruct me in your statutes. *Refrain*

13 With my lips will I recite *
      all the judgments of your mouth.
14 I have taken greater delight in the way of
      your decrees *
      than in all manner of riches. *Refrain*

15 I will meditate on your commandments *
      and give attention to your ways.
16 My delight is in your statutes; *
      I will not forget your word. *Refrain*

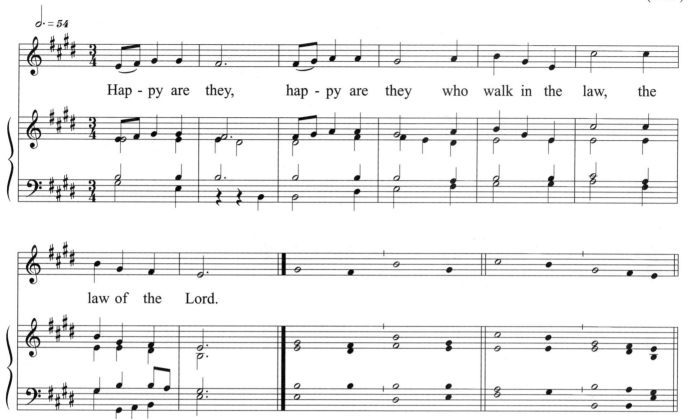

Hap - py are they, hap - py are they who walk in the law, the

law of the Lord.

1 Happy are they whose way is blameless, *
   who walk in the law of the Lord!
2 Happy are they who observe his decrees *
   and seek him with all their hearts!
      Refrain

3 Who never do any wrong, *
   but always walk in his ways.
4 You laid down your commandments, *
   that we should fully keep them. *Refrain*

5 Oh, that my ways were made so direct *
   that I might keep your statutes!
6 Then I should not be put to shame, *
   when I regard all your commandments.
      Refrain
7 I will thank you with an unfeigned heart, *
   when I have learned your
   righteous judgments.
8 I will keep your statutes; *
   do not utterly forsake me. *Refrain*

9 How shall a young man cleanse his way? *
   By keeping to your words.
10 With my whole heart I seek you; *
   let me not stray from your commandments.
      Refrain
11 I treasure your promise in my heart, *
   that I may not sin against you.
12 Blessed are you, O Lord; *
   instruct me in your statutes. *Refrain*

13 With my lips will I recite *
   all the judgments of your mouth.
14 I have taken greater delight in the way of
   your decrees *
   than in all manner of riches. *Refrain*

15 I will meditate on your commandments *
   and give attention to your ways.
16 My delight is in your statutes; *
   I will not forget your word. *Refrain*

Psalm 122

RCL Psalm 122
BCP Psalm 122

Advent 1A
Advent 1A, Lent 4B

I was glad when they said to me, "Let us go to the house of the Lord."

2 Now our feet are standing *
    within your gates, O Jerusalem.
                       Refrain

3 Jerusalem is built as a city *
    that is at unity with itself;

4 To which the tribes go up,
    the tribes of the Lord, *
        the assembly of Israel,
        to praise the Name of the Lord.

5 For there are the thrones of judgment, *
    the thrones of the house of David.
                 Refrain

6 Pray for the peace of Jerusalem: *
    "May they prosper who love you.

7 Peace be within your walls *
    and quietness within your towers.
                 Refrain

8 For my brethren and companions' sake, *
    I pray for your prosperity.

9 Because of the house of the Lord our God, *
    I will seek to do you good."   *Refrain*

Our eyes look to the Lord our God, plead-ing for his mer - cy.

1   To you I lift up my eyes, *
        to you enthroned in the heavens.
2   As the eyes of servants look to the hand of their masters, *
        and the eyes of a maid to the hand of her mistress,
3   So our eyes look to the Lord our God, *
        until he show us his mercy.   *Refrain*

4   Have mercy upon us, O Lord, have mercy, *
        for we have had more than enough of contempt,
5   Too much of the scorn of the indolent rich, *
        and of the derision of the proud.   *Refrain*

Psalm 126

RCL Psalm 126   Advent 3B, Proper 25B, Thanksgiving Day B, Lent 5C

BCP Psalm 126   Easter Vigil ABC, Advent 3B, Advent 2C, Lent 5C

The Lord has done great things for us and we are glad in-deed. The Lord has done great things for us and we are glad, and we are glad in-deed.

1   When the Lord restored the fortunes of Zion, *
     then were we like those who dream.

2   Then was our mouth filled with laughter, *
     and our tongue with shouts of joy.

3   Then they said among the nations, *
     "The Lord has done great things for them."
                            Refrain

5   Restore our fortunes, O Lord, *
     like the watercourses of the Negev.

6   Those who sowed with tears *
     will reap with songs of joy.

7   Those who go out weeping, carrying the seed, *
     will come again with joy, shouldering
     their sheaves.
                            Refrain

Tune: *Puer natus in Bethlehem,* German, 16th Century, L. Lossius's *Psalmodia,* 1553.
From *The Portland Psalter* © 2002, Robert A. Hawthorne. Church Publishing Incorporated. All rights reserved.

The Lord bless you from Zi - on all the days, the days of your life.

1   Happy are they all who fear the Lord, *
        and who follow in his ways!

2   You shall eat the fruit of your labor; *
        happiness and prosperity shall be yours.

                                        Refrain

3   Your wife shall be like a fruitful
    vine within your house, *
        your children like olive shoots
        round about your table.

4   The man who fears the Lord *
        shall thus indeed be blessed.   *Refrain*

5   The Lord bless you from Zion, *
        and may you see the prosperity of
        Jerusalem all the days of your life.

6   May you live to see your children's children; *
        may peace be upon Israel.   *Refrain*

Psalm 130

RCL Psalm 130
BCP Psalm 130

Lent 5A, Proper 5B, Proper 8B, Proper 14B
Lent 5A, Epiphany 3B, Proper 5B

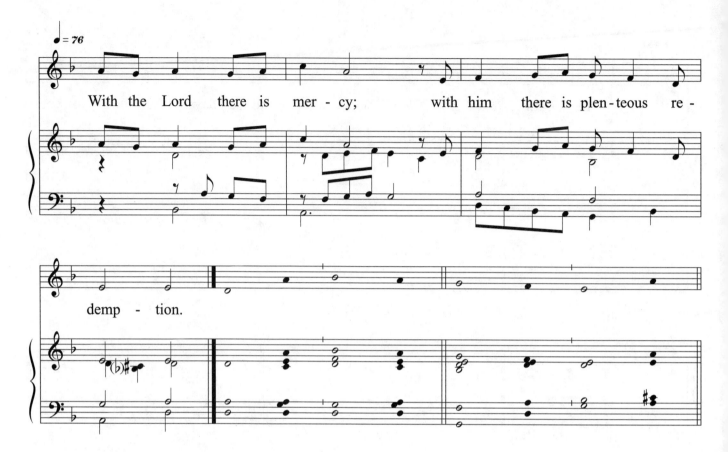

♩ = 76

With the Lord there is mer - cy; with him there is plen - teous re -

demp - tion.

1   Out of the depths have I called to you, O Lord;
Lord, hear my voice; *
      let your ears consider well the voice
      of my supplication.   *Refrain*

2   If you, Lord, were to note what is done amiss, *
      O Lord, who could stand?
3   For there is forgiveness with you; *
      therefore you shall be feared.   *Refrain*

4   I wait for the Lord; my soul waits for him; *
      in his word is my hope
5   My soul waits for the Lord,
more than watchmen for the morning, *
      more than watchmen for the morning.
                          Refrain

6   O Israel, wait for the Lord, *
      for with the Lord there is mercy;
7   With him there is plenteous redemption, *
      and he shall redeem Israel from all their sins.
                          Refrain

RCL Psalm 132:1-13, (14-19)   Proper 29B
BCP Psalm 132   Advent 4B

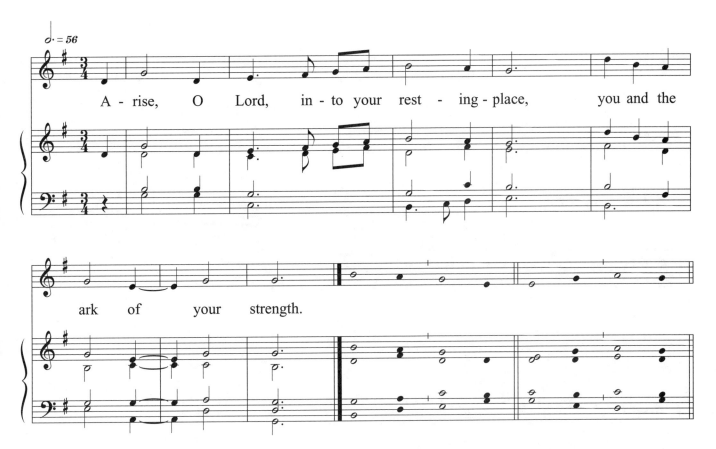

A - rise, O Lord, in-to your rest - ing-place, you and the ark of your strength.

1 Lord, remember David, *
    and all the hardships he endured;
2 How he swore an oath to the Lord *
    and vowed a vow to the Mighty One
    of Jacob: *Refrain*
3 "I will not come under the roof of my house," *
    nor climb up into my bed;
4 I will not allow my eyes to sleep, *
    nor let my eyelids slumber;
5 Until I find a place for the Lord, *
    a dwelling for the Mighty One of Jacob."
                                     Refrain
6 "The ark! We heard it was in Ephrathah; *
    we found it in the fields of Jearim.
7 Let us go to God's dwelling place; *
    let us fall upon our knees before his
    footstool."   *Refrain*

9 Let your priests be clothed with righteousness; *
    let your faithful people sing with joy.
10 For your servant David's sake, *
    do not turn away the face of your
    Anointed.   *Refrain*

11 The Lord has sworn an oath to David; *
    in truth, he will not break it:
12 "A son, the fruit of your body *
    will I set upon your throne.
13 If your children keep my covenant
    and my testimonies that I shall teach them, *
    their children will sit upon your throne
    for evermore."   *Refrain*
14 For the Lord has chosen Zion; *
    he has desired her for his habitation:
15 "This shall be my resting-place for ever; *
    here will I dwell, for I delight in her.
                                     Refrain
16 I will surely bless her provisions, *
    and satisfy her poor with bread.
17 I will clothe her priests with salvation, *
    and her faithful people will rejoice
    and sing.   *Refrain*
18 There will I make the horn of David flourish; *
    I have prepared a lamp for my Anointed.
19 As for his enemies, I will clothe them
    with shame; *
    but as for him, his crown will shine."
                                     Refrain

Psalm 133

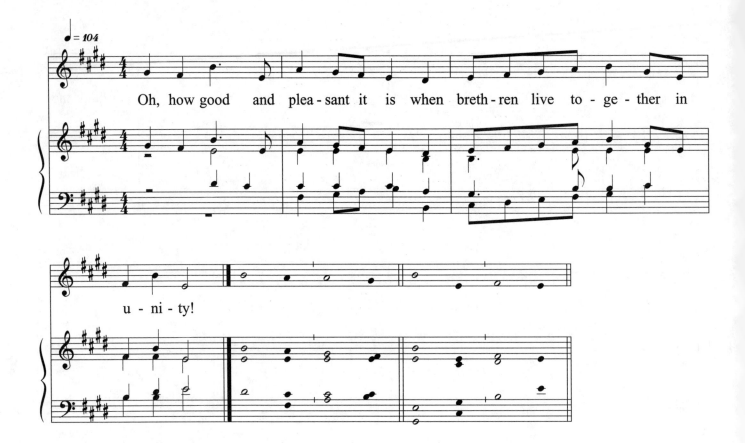

Oh, how good and plea-sant it is when breth-ren live to-ge-ther in u-ni-ty!

2 It is like fine oil upon the head *
      that runs down upon the beard,
3 Upon the beard of Aaron, *
      and runs down upon the collar of his robe.
                              Refrain
4 It is like the dew of Hermon *
      that falls upon the hills of Zion.
5 For there the Lord has ordained the blessing: *
      life for evermore.   *Refrain*

Psalm 138
(Give thanks to the Lord)

Give thanks to the Lord, who cares for the low - ly.

1 I will give thanks to you, O Lord, with
my whole heart; *
    before the gods I will sing your praise.
                Refrain

2 I will bow down toward your holy temple
and praise your Name, *
    because of your love and faithfulness;

3 For you have glorified your Name *
    and your word above all things.

4 When I called, you answered me; *
    you increased my strength within me.
                Refrain

5 All the kings of the earth will praise you,
O Lord, *
    when they have heard the words of
    your mouth.

6 They will sing of the ways of the Lord, *
    that great is the glory of the Lord.

7 Though the Lord be high, he cares
for the lowly; *
    he perceives the haughty from afar.
                Refrain

8 Though I walk in the midst of trouble,
you keep me safe; *
    you stretch forth your hand against the
    fury of my enemies; your right hand shall
    save me.

9 The Lord will make good his purpose for me; *
    O Lord, your love endures for ever;
    do not abandon the works of your hands.
                Refrain

Psalm 138

RCL Psalm 138
BCP Psalm 138

Proper 16A, Proper 5B, Epiphany 5C
Proper 16A

(O Lord, your love)

O Lord, your love en - dures for ev - er; do not a - ban - don the works

of your hands.

1   I will give thanks to you, O Lord, with
my whole heart; *
     before the gods I will sing your praise.
Refrain

2   I will bow down toward your holy temple
and praise your Name, *
     because of your love and faithfulness;

3   For you have glorified your Name *
     and your word above all things.

4   When I called, you answered me; *
     you increased my strength within me.
Refrain

5   All the kings of the earth will praise you,
O Lord, *
     when they have heard the words of
your mouth.

6   They will sing of the ways of the Lord, *
     that great is the glory of the Lord.

7   Though the Lord be high, he cares
for the lowly; *
     he perceives the haughty from afar.
Refrain

8   Though I walk in the midst of trouble,
you keep me safe; *
     you stretch forth your hand against the
fury of my enemies; your right hand shall
save me.

9   The Lord will make good his purpose for me; *
     O Lord, your love endures for ever;
     do not abandon the works of your hands.
Refrain

94

Psalm 138

(When I called you answered me)

1 I will give thanks to you, O Lord, with
my whole heart; *
> before the gods I will sing your praise.
> *Refrain*

2 I will bow down toward your holy temple
and praise your Name, *
> because of your love and faithfulness;

3 For you have glorified your Name *
> and your word above all things.

4 When I called, you answered me; *
> you increased my strength within me.
> *Refrain*

5 All the kings of the earth will praise you,
O Lord, *
> when they have heard the words of
> your mouth.

6 They will sing of the ways of the Lord, *
> that great is the glory of the Lord.

7 Though the Lord be high, he cares
for the lowly; *
> he perceives the haughty from afar.
> *Refrain*

8 Though I walk in the midst of trouble,
you keep me safe; *
> you stretch forth your hand against the
> fury of my enemies; your right hand shall
> save me.

9 The Lord will make good his purpose for me; *
> O Lord, your love endures for ever;
> do not abandon the works of your hands.
> *Refrain*

Psalm 139

RCL Psalm 139:1-11, 22-23
RCL Psalm 139:1-5, 12-17
(RCL)   **RCL** Psalm 139:1-5, 12-17

Proper 11A
Epiphany 2B
Proper 4B, Proper 18C

♩ = 60

Lord,   you   have searched   me   out   and   known   me.

1   Lord, you have searched me out and
    known me; *
        you know my sitting down and my rising
        up; you discern my thoughts from afar.
2   You trace my journeys and my resting-places *
        and are acquainted with all my ways.
3   Indeed, there is not a word on my lips, *
        but you, O Lord, know it altogether.
                                Refrain
4   You press upon me behind and before *
        and lay your hand upon me.
5   Such knowledge is too wonderful for me; *
        it is so high that I cannot attain to it.
                                Refrain
6   Where can I go then from your Spirit? *
        where can I flee from your presence?
7   If I climb up to heaven, you are there; *
        if I make the grave my bed, you are
        there also.   *Refrain*

8   If I take the wings of the morning *
        and dwell in the uttermost parts of the sea,
9   Even there your hand will lead me *
        and your right hand hold me fast.
                                Refrain
10 If I say, "Surely the darkness will cover me, *
        and the light around me turn to night,"
11 Darkness is not dark to you;
    the night is as bright as the day; *
        darkness and light to you are both alike.
                                Refrain
12 For you yourself created my inmost parts; *
        you knit me together in my mother's womb.
13 I will thank you because I am marvelously made; *
        your works are wonderful,
        and I know it well.   *Refrain*

Text continues on next page

Lord,   you   have searched me   out   and   known   me.

14 My body was not hidden from you, *
     while I was being made in secret
     and woven in the depths of the earth.

15 Your eyes beheld my limbs, yet unfinished in the womb;
   all of them were written in your book; *
     they were fashioned day by day,
     when as yet there was none of them.
                      Refrain

16 How deep I find your thoughts, O God! *
   how great is the sum of them!

17 If I were to count them, they would be
   more in number than the sand; *
     to count them all, my life span
     would need to be like yours.   *Refrain*

22 Search me out, O God, and know my heart; *
   try me and know my restless thoughts.

23 Look well whether there be any wickedness in me *
   and lead me in the way that is everlasting.
                     Refrain

Psalm 145

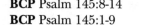

RCL Psalm 145:8-15	Proper 9A
RCL Psalm 145:10-19	Proper 12B
BCP Psalm 145:8-14	Proper 9A
BCP Psalm 145:1-9	Easter 5C

I will ex-alt you, O God my King, and bless your Name for ev - er

and ev - er.

2 Every day will I bless you *
      and praise your Name for ever and ever.

3 Great is the Lord and greatly to be praised; *
      there is no end to his greatness. *Refrain*

4 One generation shall praise your
   works to another *
      and shall declare your power.

5 I will ponder the glorious splendor
   of your majesty *
      and all your marvelous works. *Refrain*

6 They shall speak of the might of your
   wondrous acts, *
      and I will tell of your greatness.

7 They shall publish the remembrance of
   your great goodness; *
      they shall sing of your righteous deeds.
                                          Refrain

8 The Lord is gracious and full of compassion, *
      slow to anger and of great kindness.

9 The Lord is loving to everyone *
      and his compassion is over all his works.
                                          Refrain

10 All your works praise you, O Lord, *
      and your faithful servants bless you.

11 They make known the glory of your kingdom *
      and speak of your power;

12 That the peoples may know of your power *
      and the glorious splendor of your kingdom.

13 Your kingdom is an everlasting kingdom; *
      your dominion endures throughout all ages.
                                          Refrain

14 The Lord is faithful in all his words *
      and merciful in all his deeds.

15 The Lord upholds all those who fall; *
      he lifts up those who are bowed down.
                                          Refrain

16 The eyes of all wait upon you, O Lord, *
      and you give them their food in due season.

17 You open wide your hand *
      and satisfy the needs of every living creature.
                                          Refrain

18 The Lord is righteous in all his ways *
      and loving in all his works.

19 The Lord is near to those who call upon him, *
      to all who call upon him faithfully.
                                          Refrain

Psalm 146

1   Hallelujah!
    Praise the Lord, O my soul! *
        I will praise the Lord as long as I live;
        I will sing praises to my God while I
        have my being.   *Refrain*

2   Put not your trust in rulers, nor in any
    child of earth, *
        for there is no help in them.

3   When they breathe their last, they
    return to earth, *
        and in that day their thoughts perish.
                                          Refrain

4   Happy are they who have the God of Jacob
    for their help! *
        whose hope is in the Lord their God;

5   Who made heaven and earth, the seas, and
    all that is in them; *
        who keeps his promise for ever;

6   Who gives justice to those who
    are oppressed, *
        and food to those who hunger. *Refrain*

7   The Lord sets the prisoners free;
    the Lord opens the eyes of the blind; *
        the Lord lifts up those who are bowed down;

8   The Lord loves the righteous;
    the Lord cares for the stranger; *
        he sustains the orphan and widow,
        but frustrates the way of the wicked.
                                          Refrain

9   The Lord shall reign for ever, *
        your God, O Zion, throughout all
        generations. Hallelujah!   *Refrain*

Psalm 147

RCL Psalm 147:1-12, 21c

Epiphany 5B

How pleas-ant it is to ho-nor God with praise, hal-le-lu-jah.

1 Hallelujah!
   How good it is to sing praises to our God! *
      how pleasant it is to honor him with
      praise!
2 The Lord rebuilds Jerusalem; *
      he gathers the exiles of Israel.
3 He heals the brokenhearted *
      and binds up their wounds.   *Refrain*

4 He counts the number of the stars *
      and calls them all by their names.
5 Great is our Lord and mighty in power; *
      there is no limit to his wisdom.   *Refrain*

6 The Lord lifts up the lowly, *
      but casts the wicked to the ground.
7 Sing to the Lord with thanksgiving; *
      make music to our God upon the harp.
                                        Refrain

8 He covers the heavens with clouds *
      and prepares rain for the earth;
9 He makes grass to grow upon the mountains *
      and green plants to serve mankind.
10 He provides food for flocks and herds *
      and for the young ravens when they cry.
                                        Refrain
11 He is not impressed by the might of a horse; *
      he has no pleasure in the strength of a
      man;
12 But the Lord has pleasure in those who
   fear him, *
      in those who await his gracious favor.
21   Hallelujah!   *Refrain*

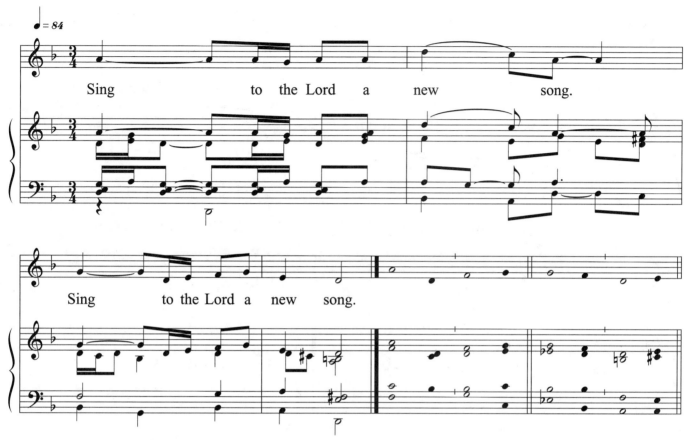

Sing to the Lord a new song.

Sing to the Lord a new song.

1   Hallelujah!
    Praise the Lord from the heavens; *
        praise him in the heights.
2   Praise him, all you angels of his; *
        praise him, all his host.   *Refrain*

3   Praise him, sun and moon; *
        praise him, all you shining stars.
4   Praise him, heaven of heavens, *
        and you waters above the heavens.
                                          Refrain
5   Let them praise the Name of the Lord; *
        for he commanded, and they were
        created.
6   He made them stand fast for ever and ever; *
        he gave them a law which shall
        not pass away.   *Refrain*

7   Praise the Lord from the earth, *
        you sea-monsters and all deeps;
8   Fire and hail, snow and fog, *
        tempestuous wind, doing his will;

                                          Refrain

9   Mountains and all hills, *
        fruit trees and all cedars;
10 Wild beasts and all cattle, *
        creeping things and winged birds;
                                          Refrain
11 Kings of the earth and all peoples, *
        princes and all rulers of the world;
12 Young men and maidens, *
        old and young together.   *Refrain*

13 Let them praise the Name of the Lord, *
    for his Name only is exalted,
        his splendor is over earth and heaven.
14 He has raised up strength for his people
    and praise for all his loyal servants, *
        the children of Israel, a people who
        are near him.
    Hallelujah!   *Refrain*

101

Psalm 149

Sing to the Lord a new song.

Sing to the Lord a new song.

1   Hallelujah!
    Sing to the Lord a new song; *
        sing his praise in the congregation
        of the faithful.   *Refrain*

2   Let Israel rejoice in his Maker; *
        let the children of Zion be joyful
        in their King.

3   Let them praise his Name in the dance; *
        let them sing praise to him with
        timbrel and harp.   *Refrain*

4   For the Lord takes pleasure in his people *
        and adorns the poor with victory.

5   Let the faithful rejoice in triumph; *
        let them be joyful on their beds. *Refrain*

6   Let the praises of God be in their throat *
        and a two-edged sword in their hand;

7   To wreak vengeance on the nations *
        and punishment on the peoples;

8   To bind their kings in chains *
        and their nobles with links of iron;

9   To inflict on them the judgment decreed; *
        this is glory for all his faithful people.
        Hallelujah!   *Refrain*

RCL Luke 1:46-55   Advent 3A, Advent 3B, Advent 4B
BCP Luke 1:46-55   Advent 3B

Canticle 15

The Song of Mary *Magnificat*

My soul proclaims the greatness of the
Lord, my spirit rejoices in God my Savior; *
    for he has looked with favor on his
    lowly servant.
From this day all generations will call me
blessed: *
    the Almighty has done great things for
    me, and holy is his Name.   *Refrain*

He has mercy on those who fear him *
    in every generation.
He has shown the strength of his arm, *
    he has scattered the proud in their
    conceit.   *Refrain*

He has cast down the mighty from their
thrones, *
    and has lfted up the lowly.
He has filled the hungry with good things, *
    and the rich he has sent away empty.
                        Refrain

He has come to the help of his servant
Israel, *
    for he has remembered his promise of
    mercy,
The promise he made to our fathers, *
    to Abraham and his children for ever.
                        Refrain
Glory to the Father, and to the Son, and to
the Holy Spirit: *
    as it was in the beginning, is now, and
    will be for ever. Amen.   *Refrain*

Index for Revised Common Lectionary Psalms

Page	RCL	Liturgical Use	Year	Year	Year	Refrain Text
1	1	Proper 25	A			Happy are they whose delight is in the law of the Lord.
	1	Easter 7		B		Happy are they whose delight is in the law of the Lord.
	1	Proper 20		B		Happy are they whose delight is in the law of the Lord.
	1	Epiphany 6			C	Happy are they whose delight is in the law of the Lord.
	1	Proper 1			C	Happy are they whose delight is in the law of the Lord.
	1	Proper 18			C	Happy are they whose delight is in the law of the Lord.
2	8	Holy Name	A	B	C	How exalted is your Name, O Lord, in all the world.
	8	New Year's Day	A	B	C	How exalted is your Name, O Lord, in all the world.
	8	Trinity Sunday	A		C	How exalted is your Name, O Lord, in all the world.
	8	Proper 22		B		How exalted is your Name, O Lord, in all the world.
3	13	Proper 8	A			Give light to my eyes, O Lord.
4	15	Epiphany 4	A			The righteous shall abide upon God's holy hill.
	15	Proper 17		B		The righteous shall abide upon God's holy hill.
	15	Proper 11			C	The righteous shall abide upon God's holy hill.
5	16	Easter 2	A			The Lord will show you the path of life.
	16	Proper 28		B		The Lord will show you the path of life.
	16	Proper 8			C	The Lord will show you the path of life.
6	19	Lent 3		B		Let the words of my mouth and the meditation of my heart be acceptable in your sight.
7	19	Easter Vigil	A	B	C	The statutes of the Lord rejoice the heart.
	19	Proper 22	A			The statutes of the Lord rejoice the heart.
	19	Proper 19		B		The statutes of the Lord rejoice the heart.
	19:7-14	Proper 21		B		The statutes of the Lord rejoice the heart.
8	22	Good Friday	A	B	C	My God, my God, why have you forsaken me?
9	22:22-30	Lent 2		B		All the ends of the earth shall remember and turn to the Lord.

Page	RCL	Liturgical Use	Year	Year	Year	Refrain Text
9	22:24-30	Easter 5		B		All the ends of the earth shall remember and turn to the Lord.
	22:18-27	Proper 7			C	All the ends of the earth shall remember and turn to the Lord.
10	23	Lent 4	A			The Lord is my Shepherd, I shall not be in want.
	23	Easter 4	A	B	C	The Lord is my Shepherd, I shall not be in want.
	23	Proper 11		B		The Lord is my Shepherd, I shall not be in want.
11	24	Proper 10		B		Lift up your heads, O gates; and the King of glory shall come in.
12	25:1-9	Lent 1		B		Lead me in your truth, O Lord and teach me.
14	27:1,5-13	Epiphany 3	A			The Lord is my light and my salvation.
	27	Lent 2			C	The Lord is my light and my salvation.
16	29	Epiphany 1	A	B	C	Worship the Lord in his holy temple.
	29	Trinity Sunday		B		Worship the Lord in his holy temple.
17	30	Epiphany 6		B		O Lord my God, I cried out to you, and you restored me to health.
	30	Proper 1		B		O Lord my God, I cried out to you, and you restored me to health.
	30	Proper 8		B		O Lord my God, I cried out to you, and you restored me to health.
	30	Proper 5			C	O Lord my God, I cried out to you, and you restored me to health.
	30	Proper 9			C	O Lord my God, I cried out to you, and you restored me to health.
18	31:1-5, 15-16	Holy Saturday	A	B	C	Into your hands, O Lord, I commend my spirit.
	31:9-16	Palm Sunday: Eucharist	A	B	C	Into your hands, O Lord, I commend my spirit.
20	32	Lent 1	A			Happy are they whose transgressions are forgiven; and whose sin is put away.
	32	Lent 4			C	Happy are they whose transgressions are forgiven; and whose sin is put away.
21	32	Proper 6			C	I acknowledge my sin to you, and you forgave me the guilt of my sin.
	32:1-8	Proper 26			C	I acknowledge my sin to you, and you forgave me the guilt of my sin.
24	33:12-22	Proper 14			C	Our soul waits for the Lord; he is our help and our shield.
26	34:1-10, 22	All Saints' Day	A			Taste and see that the Lord is good.
	34:1-8	Proper 14		B		Taste and see that the Lord is good.

Page	RCL	Liturgical Use	Year	Year	Year	Refrain Text
26	34:1-8, (19-22)	Proper 25		B		Taste and see that the Lord is good.
27	34:9-14	Proper 15		B		Taste and see that the Lord is good.
	34:15-22	Proper 16		B		Taste and see that the Lord is good.
28	37:1-12, 41-42	Epiphany 7			C	Put your trust in the Lord and do good.
	37:1-18	Proper 2			C	Put your trust in the Lord and do good.
	37:1-10	Proper 22			C	Put your trust in the Lord and do good.
30	40:1-12	Epiphany 2	A			Behold, I come to do your will, O God.
31	41	Epiphany 7		B		Happy are they who have given to the poor.
32	42	Easter Vigil	A	B	C	As the deer longs for the waterbrooks, so longs my soul for you, O God.
	42	Proper 7			C	As the deer longs for the waterbrooks, so longs my soul for you, O God.
33	43	Easter Vigil	A	B	C	Send out your light and your truth that they may lead me.
	43	Proper 26	A			Send out your light and your truth that they may lead me.
	43	Proper 7			C	Send out your light and your truth that they may lead me.
34	46	Easter Vigil	A	B	C	The Lord of hosts is with us; the God of Jacob is our stronghold.
	46	Proper 4	A			The Lord of hosts is with us; the God of Jacob is our stronghold.
	46	Proper 29			C	The Lord of hosts is with us; the God of Jacob is our stronghold.
35	47	Ascension Day	A	B	C	God has gone up with a shout, the Lord with the sound of the ram's horn.
	47	Easter 7	A	B	C	God has gone up with a shout, the Lord with the sound of the ram's horn.
36	49:1-11	Proper 13			C	We can never ransom ourselves, or deliver to God the price of our life.
37	50:1-6	Epiphany Last		B		Out of Zion, perfect in its beauty, God reveals himself in glory.
38	51:1-13	Lent 5		B		Create in me a clean heart, O God.
	51:1-11	Proper 19			C	Create in me a clean heart, O God.
39	51:1-13	Proper 13		B		Have mercy on me, O God, according to your loving kindness.
40	54	Proper 20		B		God is my helper; the Lord sustains my life.
41	62:6-14	Epiphany 3		B		For God alone my soul in silence waits.
43	65	Thanksgiving Day	A			You crown the year with your goodness, and your paths overflow with plenty.
	65	Proper 25			C	You crown the year with your goodness, and your paths overflow with plenty.

Page	RCL	Liturgical Use	Year	Year	Year	Refrain Text
44	66:7-18	Easter 6	A			Be joyful in God, all you lands.
	66:1-8; 66:10-14	Proper 9			C	Be joyful in God all you lands.
	66:1-11	Proper 23			C	Be joyful in God, all you lands.
46	67	Proper 15	A			Let the peoples praise you, O God, let all the peoples praise you.
	67	Easter 6			C	Let the peoples praise you, O God, let all the peoples praise you.
48	68:1-10, 33-36	Easter 7	A			Sing to God, O kingdoms of the earth; sing praises to the Lord.
50	72:1-7, 10-14	Epiphany	A	B	C	All kings shall bow down before him; all the nations shall do him service.
52	80:1-7, 16-18	Advent 4	A			Restore us, O God of hosts; show the light of your countenance, and we shall be saved.
	80:1-7, 16-18	Advent 1		B		Restore us, O God of hosts; show the light of your countenance, and we shall be saved.
	80:1-7	Advent 4			C	Restore us, O God of hosts; show the light of your countenance, and we shall be saved.
53	82	Proper 10			C	Arise, O God, and rule the earth, for you shall take all nations for your own.
	82	Proper 15			C	Arise, O God, and rule the earth, for you shall take all nations for your own.
54	84:1-8	Christmas 2	A	B	C	How dear to me is your dwelling, O Lord of hosts!
	84	Proper 16		B		How dear to me is your dwelling, O Lord of hosts!
	84:1-6	Proper 25			C	How dear to me is your dwelling, O Lord of hosts!
56	85:8-13	Proper 14	A			Show us your mercy, O Lord, and grant us thy salvation.
	85:1-2, 8-13	Advent 2		B		Show us your mercy, O Lord, and grant us thy salvation.
	85:8-13	Proper 10		B		Show us your mercy, O Lord, and grant us thy salvation.
	85	Proper 12			C	Show us your mercy, O Lord, and grant us thy salvation.
58	89:1-29	Epiphany 1	A	B	C	I have found David my servant; with my holy oil have I anointed him.
	89:19-37	Proper 11		B		I have found David my servant; with my holy oil have I anointed him.
60	90:1-8, (9-11), 12	Proper 28	A			Teach us to number our days that we may apply our hearts to wisdom.
61	90:12-17	Proper 23		B		Teach us to number our days that we may apply our hearts to wisdom.

Page	RCL	Liturgical Use	Year	Year	Year	Refrain Text
62	91:9-16	Proper 24		B		Because he is bound to me in love, therefore will I deliver him.
	91:1-6, 14-16	Proper 21			C	Because he is bound to me in love, therefore will I deliver him.
63	93	Ascension Day	A	B	C	The Lord shall reign for ever and ever.
	93	Easter 7	A	B	C	The Lord shall reign for ever and ever.
	93	Proper 29		B		The Lord shall reign for ever and ever.
64	95	Lent 3	A			Today if you would hear his voice, harden not your hearts.
65	96	Christmas Day 1	A	B	C	Today is born our Savior, Christ the Lord.
66	98	Christmas Day 3	A	B	C	All the ends of the earth have seen the salvation of our God.
67	98	Easter 6		B		Sing to the Lord a new song.
68	99	Epiphany Last	A		C	Proclaim the greatness of the Lord our God; he is the Holy One.
	99	Proper 24	A			Proclaim the greatness of the Lord our God, he is the Holy One.
69	100	Proper 6	A			We are his people and the sheep of his pasture.
	100	Thanksgiving Day			C	We are his people and the sheep of his pasture.
70	103:(1-7), 8-13	Proper 19	A			The Lord is full of compassion and mercy, slow to anger and of great kindness.
	103:1-13, 22	Epiphany 8		B		The Lord is full of compassion and mercy, slow to anger and of great kindness.
	103:1-13, 22	Proper 3		B		The Lord is full of compassion and mercy, slow to anger and of great kindness.
	103:1-8	Proper 16			C	The Lord is full of compassion and mercy, slow to anger and of great kindness.
71	103:8-14	Ash Wednesday	A	B	C	The Lord remembers that we are but dust.
72	104:25-35, 37	Vigil of Pentecost	A	B	C	Send forth your Spirit, O Lord, and renew the face of the earth.
	104:25-35, 37	Day of Pentecost	A	B	C	Send forth your Spirit, O Lord, and renew the face of the earth.
73	106:1-6, 19-23	Proper 23	A			Give thanks to the Lord, for he is good, and his mercy endures for ever.
74	107:1-7, 33-37	Proper 26	A			Give thanks to the Lord, for he is good, and his mercy endures for ever.
	107:1-3, 17-22	Lent 4		B		Give thanks to the Lord, for he is good, and his mercy endures for ever.
	107:1-3, 23-32	Proper 7		B		Give thanks to the Lord, for he is good; and his mercy endures for ever.
	107:1-9, 43	Proper 13			C	Give thanks to the Lord, for he is good, and his mercy endures for ever.

Page	RCL	Liturgical Use	Year	Year	Year	Refrain Text
77	112:1-9 (10)	Epiphany 5	A			Happy are they who have given to the poor.
78	114	Easter Vigil: Eucharist	A	B	C	Hallelujah, hallelujah, hallelujah!
	114	Easter Day: Evening	A	B	C	Hallelujah, hallelujah, hallelujah!
80	116:1, 10-17	Maundy Thursday	A	B	C	I will lift up the cup of salvation and call upon the Name of the Lord.
81	116:1-3, 10-17	Easter 3	A			I will walk in the presence of the Lord in the land of the living.
	116:1, 10-17	Proper 6	A			I will walk in the presence of the Lord in the land of the living.
	116:1-8	Proper 19		B		I will walk in the presence of the Lord in the land of the living.
83	118:1-2, 14-24	Easter Day	A	B	C	On this day the Lord has acted; we will rejoice and be glad in it.
84	119:1-8	Epiphany 6	A			Happy are they who walk in the law of the Lord.
	119:1-8	Proper 1	A			Happy are they who walk in the law of the Lord.
	119:9-16	Lent 5		B		Happy are they who walk in the law of the Lord.
86	122	Advent 1	A			I was glad when they said to me, "let us go to the house of the Lord."
87	123	Proper 28	A			Our eyes look to the Lord our God, pleading for his mercy.
	123	Proper 9		B		Our eyes look to the Lord our God, pleading for his mercy.
88	126	Advent 3		B		The Lord has done great things for us and we are glad indeed.
	126	Proper 25		B		The Lord has done great things for us and we are glad indeed.
	126	Thanksgiving Day		B		The Lord has done great things for us and we are glad indeed.
	126	Lent 5			C	The Lord has done great things for us and we are glad indeed.
90	130	Lent 5	A			With the Lord there is mercy; with him there is plenteous redemption.
	130	Proper 5		B		With the Lord there is mercy; with him there is plenteous redemption.
	130	Proper 8		B		With the Lord there is mercy; with him there is plentious redemption.
	130	Proper 14		B		With the Lord there is mercy; with him there is plentious redemption.
91	132:1-13, (14-19)	Proper 29		B		Arise, O Lord, into your resting-place, you and the ark of your strength.

Page	RCL	Liturgical Use	Year	Year	Year	Refrain Text
92	133	Proper 15	A			Oh, how good and pleasant it is, when brethren live together in unity!
	133	Easter 2		B		Oh, how good and pleasant it is, when brethren live together in unity!
	133	Proper 7		B		Oh, how good and pleasant it is when brethren live together in unity!
94	138	Proper 16	A			O Lord, your love endures for ever; do not abandon the work of your hands.
	138	Proper 5		B		O Lord, your love endures for ever; do not abandon the work of your hands.
	138	Epiphany 5			C	O Lord, your love endures for ever; do not abandon the work of your hands.
95	138	Proper 12			C	When I called, you answered me; O Lord, your love endures for ever.
96	139:1-11, 22-23	Proper 11	A			Lord, you have searched me out and known me.
	139:1-5, 12-17	Epiphany 2		B		Lord, you have searched me out and known me.
	139:1-5, 12-17	Proper 4		B		Lord, you have searched me out and known me.
	139:1-5, 12-17	Proper 18			C	Lord, you have searched me out and known me.
98	145:8-15	Proper 9	A			I will exalt you, O God my King, and bless your Name for ever and ever.
	145:10-19	Proper 12		B		I will exalt you, O God my King, and praise your Name for ever and ever.
99	146	Proper 18		B		Praise the Lord, O my soul! I will praise the Lord as long as I live.
	146	Proper 26		B		Praise the Lord, O my soul! I will praise the Lord as long as I live.
	146	Proper 27		B		Praise the Lord, O my soul! I will praise the Lord as long as I live.
	146	Proper 5			C	Praise the Lord, O my soul! I will praise the Lord as long as I live.
	146	Proper 21			C	Praise the Lord, O my soul! I will praise the Lord as long as I live.
100	147:1-12, 21c	Epiphany 5		B		How pleasant it is to honor God with praise, hallelujah.
101	148	Easter 5			C	Sing to the Lord a new song.
102	149	Proper 18	A			Sing to the Lord a new song.
103	Canticle 15	Advent 3	A	B		My soul proclaims the greatness of the Lord.
	Canticle 15	Advent 4		B		My soul proclaims the greatness of the Lord.

Index for Book of Common Prayer Psalms

Page	BCP	Liturgical Use	Year	Year	Year	Refrain Text
1	1	Proper 25	A			Happy are they whose delight is in the law of the Lord.
	1	Epiphany 6			C	Happy are they whose delight is in the law of the Lord.
	1	Proper 1			C	Happy are they whose delight is in the law of the Lord.
	1	Proper 18			C	Happy are they whose delight is in the law of the Lord.
2	8	Holy Name	A	B	C	How exalted is your Name, O Lord, in all the world.
	8	Proper 22		B		How exalted is your Name, O Lord, in all the world.
3	13	Proper 25		B		Give light to my eyes, O Lord.
4	15	Proper 17		B		The righteous shall abide upon God's holy hill.
	15	Proper 11			C	The righteous shall abide upon God's holy hill.
5	16:5-11	Lent 2		B		The Lord will show you the path of life.
	16	Proper 16		B		The Lord will show you the path of life.
	16:5-11	Proper 28		B		The Lord will show you the path of life.
	16:5-11	Proper 8			C	The Lord will show you the path of life.
6	19:7-14	Lent 3		B		Let the words of my mouth and the meditation of my heart be acceptable in your sight.
7	19; 19:7-14	Proper 21		B		The statutes of the Lord rejoice the heart.
8	22:1-21; 22:1-11	Good Friday	A	B	C	My God, my God, why have you forsaken me?
	22:1-21; 22:1-11	Palm Sunday: Eucharist	A	B	C	My God, my God, why have you forsaken me?
10	23	Lent 4	A			The Lord is my Shepherd, I shall not be in want.
	23	Easter 4	A	B		The Lord is my Shepherd, I shall not be in want.
11	24:1-7	Advent 4	A			Lift up your heads, O gates; and the King of glory shall come in.
12	25:3-9	Lent 1		B		Lead me in your truth, O Lord and teach me.
15	27:10-18	Lent 2			C	The Lord is my light and my salvation.
	27:1-7	Epiphany 5	A			The Lord is my light and my salvation.
	27:5-11	Epiphany Last		B		The Lord is my light and my salvation.
17	30:1-6, 12-13	Proper 5			C	O Lord my God, I cried out to you, and you restored me to health.

Page	BCP	Liturgical Use	Year	Year	Year	Refrain Text
18	31:1-5	Holy Saturday	A	B	C	Into your hands, O Lord, I commend my spirit.
20	32:1-8	Epiphany 7		B		Happy are they whose transgressions are forgiven; and whose sin is put away.
	32:1-8	Proper 2		B		Happy are they whose transgressions are forgiven; and whose sin is put away.
21	32:1-8	Proper 6			C	I acknowledge my sin to you, and you forgave me the guilt of my sin.
	32:1-8	Proper 26			C	I acknowledge my sin to you, and you forgave me the guilt of my sin.
22	33:1-11	Easter 3			C	Sing to the Lord a new song.
23	33:12-22	Lent 2	A			Lord, let your lovingkindness be upon us, as we have put our trust in you.
24	33:12-15, 18-22	Proper 14			C	Our soul waits for the Lord; he is our help and our shield.
26	34:1-8	Proper 14		B		Taste and see that the Lord is good.
	34:1-8	Lent 4			C	Taste and see that the Lord is good.
27	34:9-14	Proper 15		B		Taste and see that the Lord is good.
	34:15-22	Proper 16		B		Taste and see that the Lord is good.
29	37:1-18; 37:1-6	Epiphany 4	A			Put your trust in the Lord and do good.
	37:1-18; 37:3-10	Epiphany 7			C	Put your trust in the Lord and do good.
	37:1-18; 37:3-10	Proper 2			C	Put your trust in the Lord and do good.
	37:1-18; 37:3-10	Proper 22			C	Put your trust in the Lord and do good.
30	40:1-10	Epiphany 2	A			Behold, I come to do your will, O God.
32	42:1-7	Easter Vigil	A	B	C	As the deer longs for the waterbrooks, so longs my soul for you, O God.
	42; 42:1-7	Epiphany 6		B		As the deer longs for the waterbrooks, so longs my soul for you, O God.
	42; 42:1-7	Proper 1		B		As the deer longs for the waterbrooks, so longs my soul for you, O God.
33	43	Proper 26	A			Send out your light and your truth that they may lead me.
34	46	Easter Vigil	A	B	C	The Lord of hosts is with us; the God of Jacob is our stronghold.
	46	Proper 16			C	The Lord of hosts is with us; the God of Jacob is our stronghold.
	46	Proper 29			C	The Lord of hosts is with us; the God of Jacob is our stronghold.
35	47	Ascension Day	A	B	C	God has gone up with a shout, the Lord with the sound of the ram's horn.
	47	Easter 7	A	B	C	God has gone up with a shout, the Lord with the sound of the ram's horn.

Page	BCP	Liturgical Use	Year	Year	Year	Refrain Text
36	49:1-11	Proper 13			C	We can never ransom ourselves, or deliver to God the price of our life.
37	50:1-6	Advent 1			C	Out of Zion, perfect in its beauty, God reveals himself in glory.
38	51:11-16	Lent 5		B		Create in me a clean heart, O God.
	51:1-11	Proper 19			C	Create in me a clean heart, O God.
39	51:1-13	Lent 1	A			Have mercy on me, O God, according to your lovingkindness.
40	54	Proper 20		B		God is my helper; the Lord sustains my life.
41	62:6-14	Epiphany 8	A			For God alone my soul in silence waits.
	62:6-14	Proper 3	A			For God alone my soul in silence waits.
42	63:1-8	Proper 7			C	Lord, my soul clings to you; your right hand holds me fast.
43	65:9-14	Thanksgiving Day	A	B	C	You crown the year with your goodness, and your paths overflow with plenty.
45	66:1-11; 66:1-8	Easter 5	A	B		Be joyful in God, all you lands.
	66:1-8	Proper 9			C	Be joyful in God, all you lands.
46	67	Proper 15	A			Let the peoples praise you, O God, let all the peoples praise you.
	67	Easter 6			C	Let the peoples praise you, O God, let all the peoples praise you.
49	68:1-20	Easter 7	A	B	C	Sing to God, O kingdoms of the earth; sing praises to the Lord.
50	72:1-2, 10-17	The Epiphany	A	B	C	All kings shall bow down before him; all the nations shall do him service.
51	78:14-20, 23-25	Maundy Thursday	A	B	C	Mortals ate the bread of angels, for the Lord gave them manna from heaven.
52	80:1-7	Advent 1		B		Restore us, O God of hosts; show the light of your countenance, and we shall be saved.
	80:1-7	Advent 4			C	Restore us, O God of hosts; show the light of your countenance, and we shall be saved.
53	82	Proper 15			C	Arise, O God, and rule the earth, for you shall take all nations for your own.
54	84:1-8	Christmas 2	A	B	C	How dear to me is your dwelling, O Lord of hosts!
	84:1-6	Proper 25			C	How dear to me is your dwelling, O Lord of hosts!
57	85:7-13	Advent 2		B		Show us your mercy, O Lord, and grant us thy salvation.
	85:7-13	Proper 10		B		Show us your mercy, O Lord, and grant us thy salvation.
	85:7-13	Advent 3			C	Show us your mercy, O Lord, and grant us thy salvation.

Page	BCP	Liturgical Use	Year	Year	Year	Refrain Text
58	89:1-29; 89:19-29	Epiphany 1	A	B	C	I have found David my servant; with my holy oil have I anointed him.
60	90:1-8, 12	Proper 28	A			Teach us to number our days that we may apply our hearts to wisdom.
	90:1-8, 12	Proper 23		B		Teach us to number our days that we may apply our hearts to wisdom.
62	91:9-16	Proper 24		B		Because he is bound to me in love, therefore will I deliver him.
63	93	Trinity Sunday		B		The Lord shall reign for ever and ever.
	93	Proper 29		B		The Lord shall reign for ever and ever.
64	95:6-11	Lent 3	A			Today if you would hear his voice, harden not your hearts.
65	96:1-4, 11-12	Christmas Day 1	A	B	C	Today is born our Savior, Christ the Lord.
66	98:1-6	Christmas Day 3	A	B	C	All the ends of the earth have seen the salvation of our God.
67	98:1-5	Easter 3		B		Sing to the Lord a new song.
68	99	Epiphany Last	A		C	Proclaim the greatness of the Lord our God; he is the Holy One.
69	100	Proper 6	A			We are his people and the sheep of his pasture.
	100	Easter 4		B	C	We are his people and the sheep of his pasture.
70	103:(1-7) 8-13	Proper 19	A			The Lord is full of compassion and mercy, slow to anger and of great kindness.
	103:1-6	Epiphany 8		B		The Lord is full of compassion and mercy, slow to anger and of great kindness.
	103:1-6	Proper 3		B		The Lord is full of compassion and mercy, slow to anger and of great kindness.
	103:1-11	Lent 3			C	The Lord is full of compassion and mercy, slow to anger and of great kindness.
71	103:8-14	Ash Wednesday	A	B	C	The Lord remembers that we are but dust.
72	104:25-32	Vigil of Pentecost	A	B	C	Send forth your Spirit, O Lord, and renew the face of the earth.
	104:25-37	Day of Pentecost	A	B	C	Send forth your Spirit, O Lord, and renew the face of the earth.
74	107:1-32	Proper 7		B		Give thanks to the Lord, for he is good; and his mercy endures for ever.
	107:1-3, 23-32	Proper 7		B		Give thanks to the Lord, for he is good; and his mercy endures for ever.
76	111	Easter 2	A	B	C	The Lord has sent redemption to his people, hallelujah.
77	112	Proper 8		B		Happy are they who have given to the poor.
78	114	Easter Vigil: Eucharist	A	B	C	Hallelujah, hallelujah, hallelujah!

Page	BCP	Liturgical Use	Year	Year	Year	Refrain Text
81	116:10-17	Easter 3	A			I will walk in the presence of the Lord in the land of the living.
	116:1-8	Proper 19		B		I will walk in the presence of the Lord in the land of the living.
82	118:19-24	Easter 2	A	B	C	Give thanks to the Lord, for he is good; his mercy endures for ever.
83	118:14-29	Easter Day	A	B	C	On this day the Lord has acted; we will rejoice and be glad in it.
85	119:1-16; 119:9-16	Epiphany 6	A			Happy are they who walk in the law of the Lord.
	119:1-16; 119:9-16	Proper 1	A			Happy are they who walk in the law of the Lord.
86	122	Advent 1	A			I was glad when they said to me, "let us go to the house of the Lord."
	122	Lent 4		B		I was glad when they said to me, "let us go to the house of the Lord."
87	123	Proper 9		B		Our eyes look to the Lord our God, pleading for his mercy.
88	126	Easter Vigil	A	B	C	The Lord has done great things for us and we are glad indeed.
	126	Advent 3		B		The Lord has done great things for us and we are glad indeed.
	126	Advent 2			C	The Lord has done great things for us and we are glad indeed.
	126	Lent 5			C	The Lord has done great things for us and we are glad indeed.
89	128	Proper 22		B		The Lord bless you from Zion all the days of your life.
90	130	Lent 5	A			With the Lord there is mercy; with him there is plenteous redemption.
	130	Epiphany 3		B		With the Lord there is mercy; with him there is plenteous redemption.
	130	Proper 5		B		With the Lord there is mercy; with him there is plenteous redemption.
91	132	Advent 4		B		Arise, O Lord, into your resting-place, you and the ark of your strength.
93	138	Proper 20			C	Give thanks to the Lord, who cares for the lowly.
94	138	Proper 16	A			O Lord, your love endures for ever; do not abandon the work of your hands.
95	138	Proper 12			C	When I called, you answered me; O Lord, your love endures for ever.
97	139:1-17; 139:1-11	Epiphany 3	A			Lord, you have searched me out and known me.

Page	BCP	Liturgical Use	Year	Year	Year	Refrain Text
98	145:8-14	Proper 9	A			I will exalt you, O God my King, and bless your Name for ever and ever.
	145:1-9	Easter 5			C	I will exalt you, O God my King, and bless your Name for ever and ever.
99	146:4-9	Proper 18		B		Praise the Lord, O my soul! I will praise the Lord as long as I live.
	146:4-9	Proper 27		B		Praise the Lord, O my soul! I will praise the Lord as long as I live.
	146:4-9	Proper 21			C	Praise the Lord, O my soul! I will praise the Lord as long as I live.
101	148:7-14	Easter 6	A			Sing to the Lord a new song.
102	149	All Saints' Day	A	B	C	Sing to the Lord a new song.
103	Canticle 15	Advent 3		B		My soul proclaims the greatness of the Lord.

Congregational Refrains 1- 16

Psalm 13

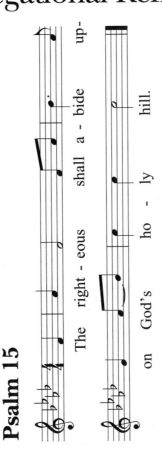

Give light, give light to my eyes, O Lord. Give light to my eyes, O Lord.

Psalm 15

The right-eous shall a-bide up-on God's ho-ly hill.

Psalm 16

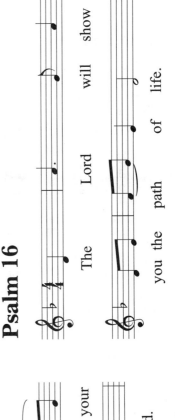

The Lord will show you the path of life.

Psalm 1

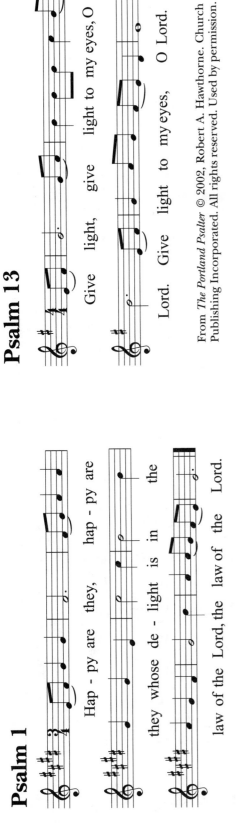

Hap-py are they, hap-py are they whose de-light is in the law of the Lord, the law of the Lord.

Psalm 8

How ex-alt-ed is your Name, O Lord, in all the world.

Congregational Refrains 19-23

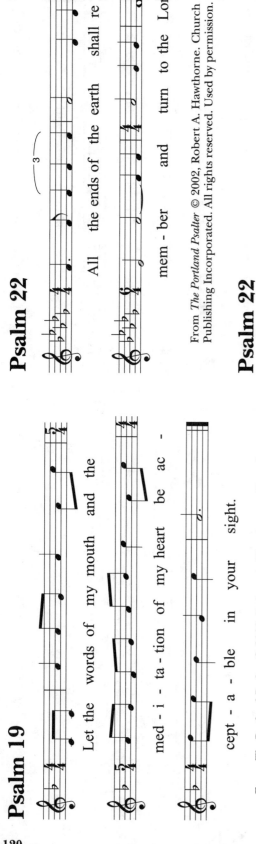

Psalm 19

Let the words of my mouth and the

med - i - ta - tion of my heart be ac -

cept - a - ble in your sight.

Psalm 19

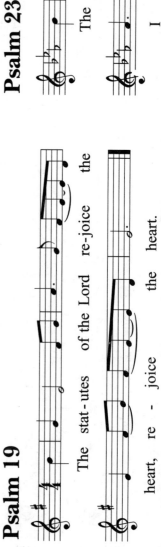

The stat - utes of the Lord re - joice the

heart, re - joice the heart.

Psalm 22

All the ends of the earth shall re -

mem - ber and turn to the Lord.

Psalm 22

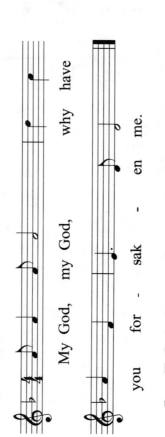

My God, my God, why have

you for - sak - en me.

Psalm 23

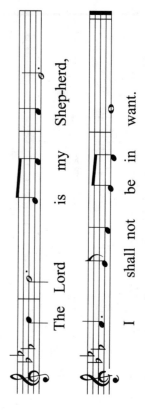

The Lord is my Shep-herd,

I shall not be in want.

Congregational Refrains 24-31

Psalm 29

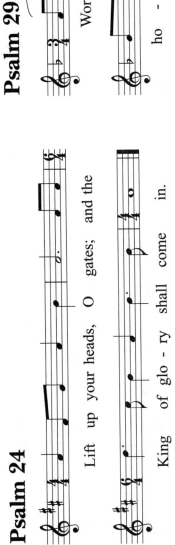

Wor-ship the Lord in his ho - ly tem - ple.

Psalm 30

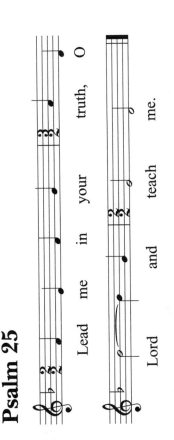

O Lord, my God, I cried out to you, and you re-stored me to health.

Psalm 31

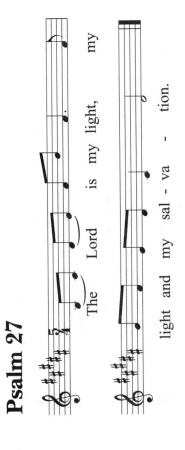

In - to your hands, O Lord, I com - mend my spir - it.

Psalm 24

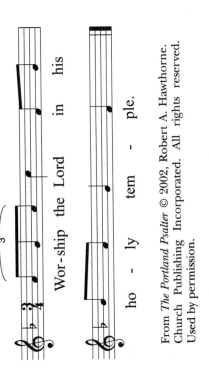

Lift up your heads, O gates; and the King of glo - ry shall come in.

Psalm 25

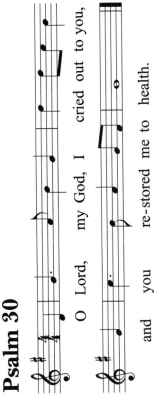

Lead me in your truth, O Lord and teach me.

Psalm 27

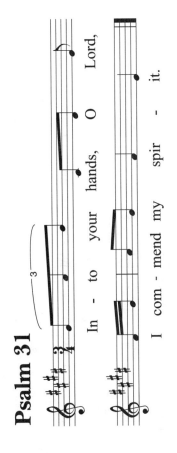

The Lord is my light, my light and my sal - va - tion.

Congregational Refrains 32-33

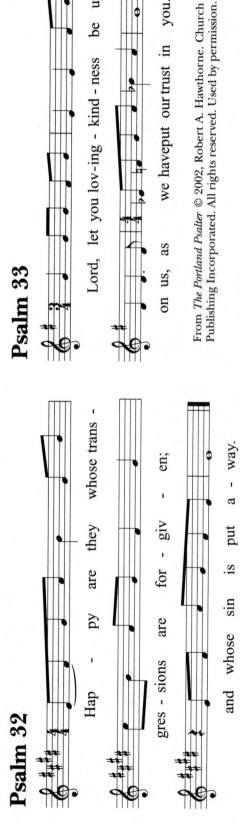

Psalm 33

Lord, let you lov-ing-kind-ness be up-on us, as we have put our trust in you.

Psalm 32

Hap-py are they whose trans-gres-sions are for-giv-en; and whose sin is put a-way.

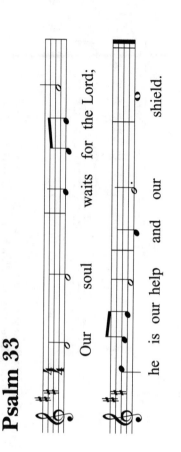

Psalm 33

Our soul waits for the Lord; he is our help and our shield.

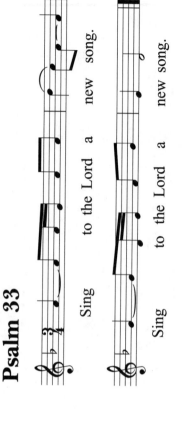

Psalm 33

Sing to the Lord a new song. Sing to the Lord a new song.

Psalm 32

I ack-now-ledge my sin to you, and you for-gave me the guilt of my sin.

Congregational Refrains 34-42

Psalm 40

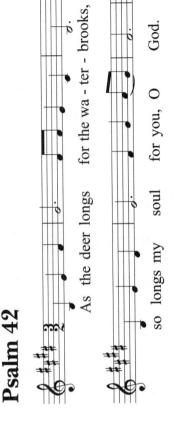

Be - hold   I come to do your
will, O God; be - hold I come.

Psalm 41

Hap - py are they who have
gi - ven, giv - en to the poor.

Psalm 42

As the deer longs for the wa - ter - brooks,
so longs my soul for you, O God.

Psalm 34

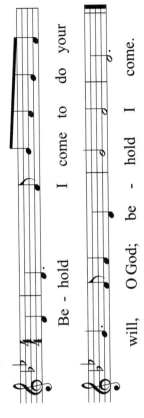

Taste and see that the Lord is good;
taste and see, taste and see.

Psalm 37

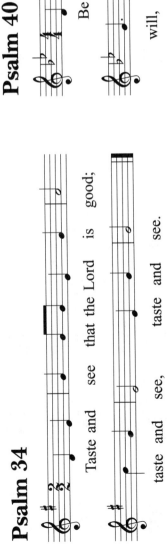

Put your trust in the Lord, put your
trust in the Lord, put your
trust in the Lord and do good.

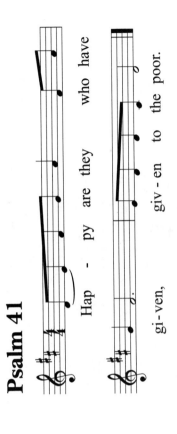

Congregational Refrains 43-51

Psalm 43

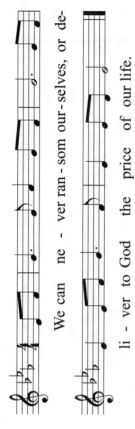

Send out your light and your truth that they may lead me.

Psalm 46

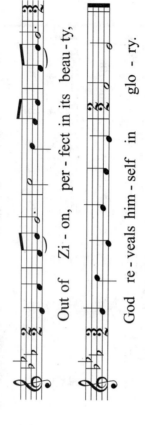

The Lord of hosts is with us; the God of Ja - cob is our strong - hold.

Psalm 47

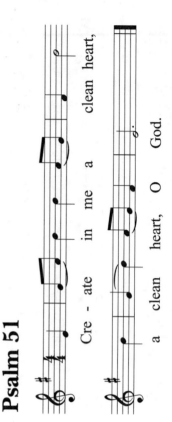

God has gone up, has gone up with a shout, the Lord with the sound of the ram's horn.

Psalm 49

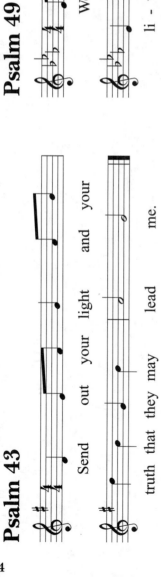

We can ne - ver ran - som our - selves, or de - li - ver to God the price of our life.

Psalm 50

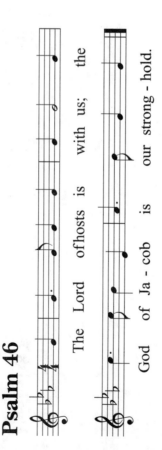

Out of Zi - on, per - fect in its beau - ty, God re - veals him - self in glo - ry.

Psalm 51

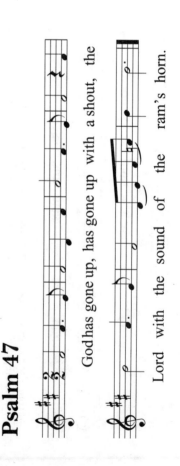

Cre - ate in me a clean heart, a clean heart, O God.

Congregational Refrains 51-66

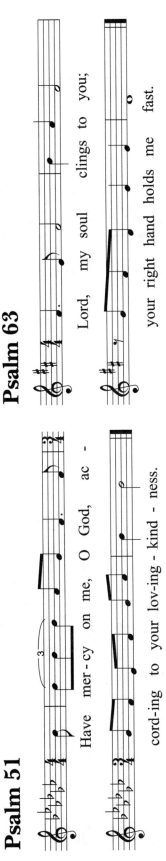

Psalm 63

Lord, my soul clings to you; your right hand holds me fast.

From *The Portland Psalter* © 2002, Robert A. Hawthorne. Church Publishing Incorporated. All rights reserved. Used by permission.

Psalm 65

You crown the year with your good-ness, and your paths o - ver - flow with plen - ty.

From *The Portland Psalter* © 2002, Robert A. Hawthorne. Church Publishing Incorporated. All rights reserved. Used by permission.

Psalm 66

Be joy - ful in God, all you lands.

From *The Portland Psalter* © 2002, Robert A. Hawthorne. Church Publishing Incorporated. All rights reserved. Used by permission.

Psalm 51

Have mer - cy on me, O God, ac - cord-ing to your lov-ing - kind - ness.

From *The Portland Psalter* © 2002, Robert A. Hawthorne. Church Publishing Incorporated. All rights reserved. Used by permission.

Psalm 54

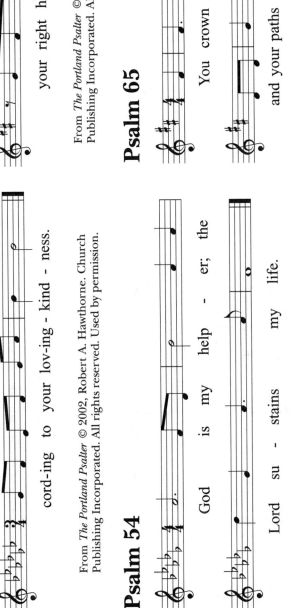

God is my help - er; the Lord su - stains my life.

From *The Portland Psalter* © 2002, Robert A. Hawthorne. Church Publishing Incorporated. All rights reserved. Used by permission.

Psalm 62

For God a - lone my soul in si - lence waits.

From *The Portland Psalter* © 2002, Robert A. Hawthorne. Church Publishing Incorporated. All rights reserved. Used by permission.

Congregational Refrains 67-80

Psalm 78

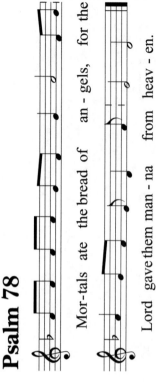

Mor-tals ate the bread of an-gels, for the Lord gave them man-na from heav-en.

Psalm 80

Re-store us, O God of hosts; show the light of your count-e-nance, and we shall be saved.

Psalm 67

Let the peo-ples praise you, O God; let all the peo-ples praise you.

Psalm 68

Sing to God, O king-doms of the earth; sing prais-es to the Lord.

Psalm 72

All kings shall bow down be-fore him; all the na-tions shall do him ser-vice.

Congregational Refrains 82-89

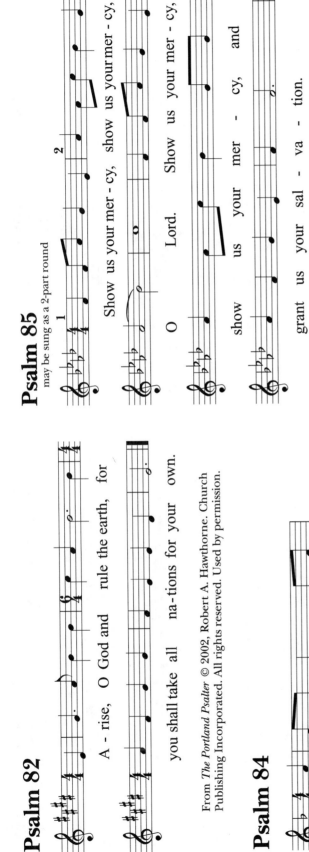

Psalm 85
may be sung as a 2-part round

Show us your mer - cy, show us your mer - cy,

Show us your mer - cy,

O Lord. Show us your mer - cy, and

show us your mer - cy, and

grant us your sal - va - tion.

Psalm 82

A - rise, O God and rule the earth, for

you shall take all na - tions for your own.

Psalm 84

How dear to me is your

dwell - ing, O Lord of hosts!

Psalm 89

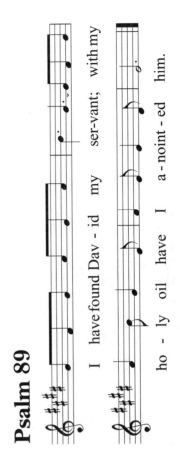

I have found Dav - id my ser - vant; with my

ho - ly oil have I a - noint - ed him.

Congregational Refrains 90-98

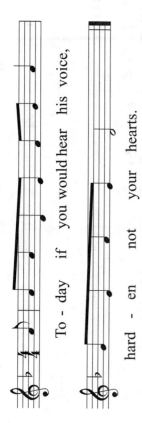

Psalm 90

Teach us to num-ber our days that
we may ap-ply our hearts to wis-dom.

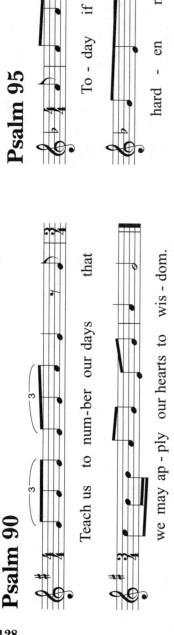

Psalm 95

To-day if you would hear his voice,
hard-en not your hearts.

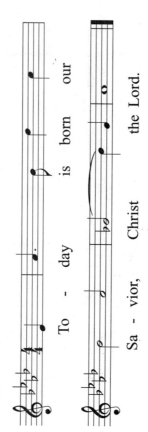

Psalm 91

Be-cause he is bound to me in love,
there-fore will I de-liv-er him.

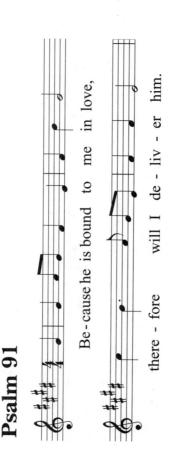

Psalm 96

To-day is born our
Sa-vior, Christ the Lord.

Psalm 93

The Lord shall reign for ev-er and ev-er.
The Lord shall reign for ev-er.

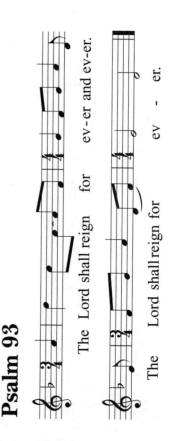

Psalm 98

Sing to the Lord a new song.
Sing to the Lord a new song.

Congregational Refrains 99-104

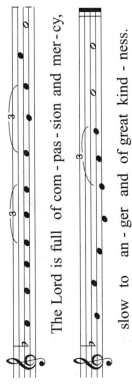

Psalm 99

Pro - claim, pro - claim the

great - ness of the Lord our God;

he is the Ho - ly One.

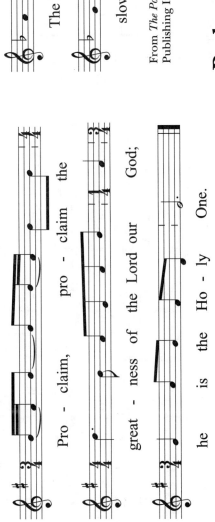

Psalm 100

We are his peo - ple

and the sheep of his pas - ture.

Psalm 103

The Lord is full of com - pas - sion and mer - cy,

slow to an - ger and of great kind - ness.

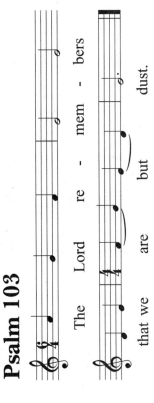

Psalm 103

The Lord re - mem - bers

that we are but dust.

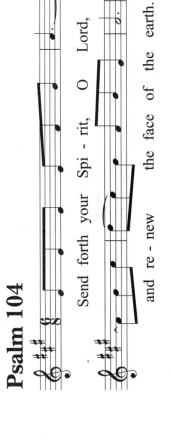

Psalm 104

Send forth your Spi - rit, O Lord,

and re - new the face of the earth.

Congregational Refrains 106-116

Psalm 106

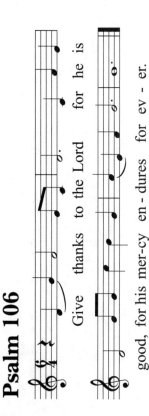

Give thanks to the Lord for he is
good, for his mer-cy en - dures for ev - er.

Psalm 107

Give thanks to the Lord for he is
good, and his mer-cy en - dures for ev - er.

Psalm 111

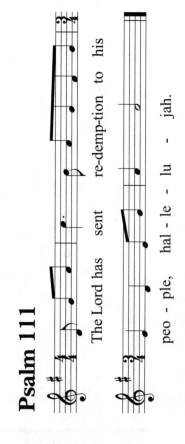

The Lord has sent re-demp-tion to his
peo - ple, hal - le - lu - jah.

Psalm 112

Hap - - py are they who have
gi - ven, giv - en to the poor.

Psalm 114

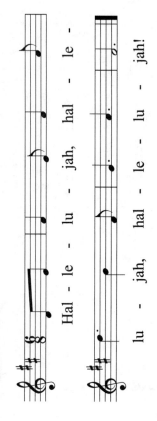

Hal - le - lu - jah, hal - le -
lu - jah, hal - le - lu - jah!

Psalm 116

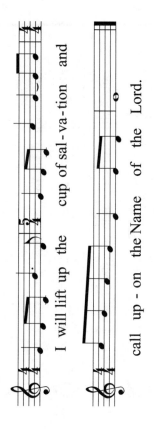

I will lift up the cup of sal - va - tion and
call up - on the Name of the Lord.

Congregational Refrains 116-123

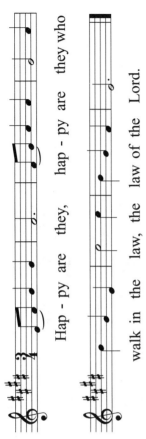

Psalm 116

I will walk in the pres-ence of the Lord,

I will walk in the land of the liv - ing.

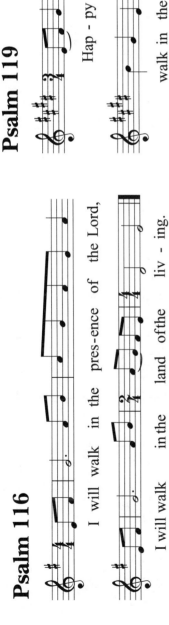

Psalm 119

Hap - py are they, hap - py are they who

walk in the law, the law of the Lord.

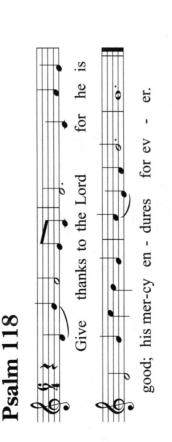

Psalm 118

Give thanks to the Lord for he is

good; his mer-cy en - dures for ev - er.

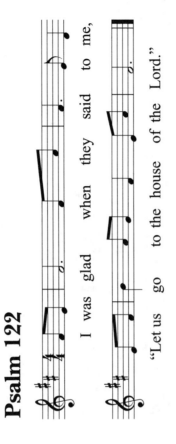

Psalm 122

I was glad when they said to me,

"Let us go to the house of the Lord."

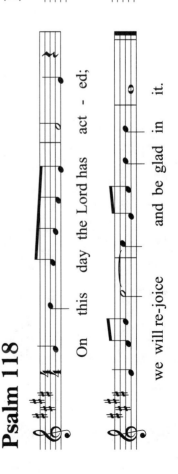

Psalm 118

On this day the Lord has act - ed;

we will re-joice and be glad in it.

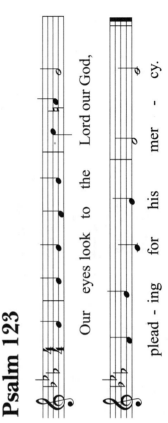

Psalm 123

Our eyes look to the Lord our God,

plead - ing for his mer - cy.

Congregational Refrains 126-133

Psalm 130

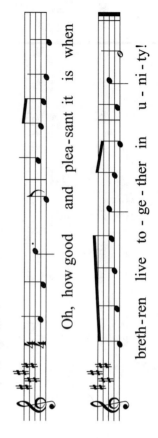

With the Lord there is mer-cy; with him there is plen-teous re-demp-tion.

Psalm 132

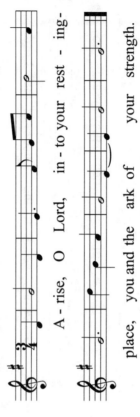

A-rise, O Lord, in-to your rest-ing-place, you and the ark of your strength.

Psalm 133

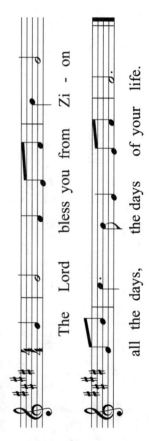

Oh, how good and plea-sant it is when breth-ren live to-ge-ther in u-ni-ty!

Psalm 126

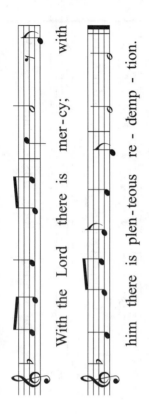

The Lord has done great things for us and we are glad in-deed. The Lord has done great things for us and we are glad, and we are glad in-deed.

Tune: *Puer natus in Bethlehem*, German, 16th Century, L. Lossius's *Psalmodia*, 1553. From *The Portland Psalter* © 2002, Robert A. Hawthorne. Church Publishing Incorporated. All rights reserved. Used by permission.

Psalm 128

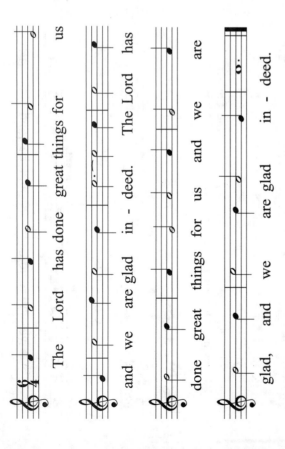

The Lord bless you from Zi-on all the days, the days of your life.

Congregational Refrains 138-146

Psalm 139

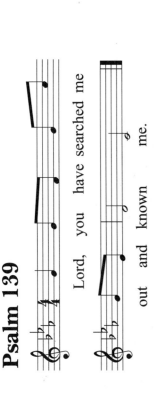

Lord, you have searched me out and known me.

Psalm 145

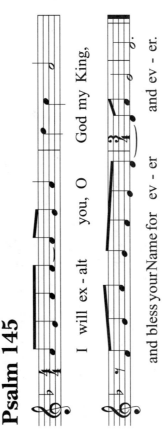

I will ex-alt you, O God my King, and bless your Name for ev-er and ev-er.

Psalm 146

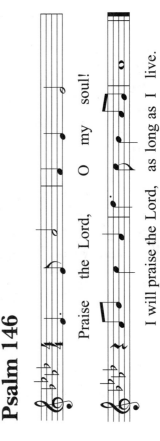

Praise the Lord, O my soul! I will praise the Lord, as long as I live.

Psalm 138

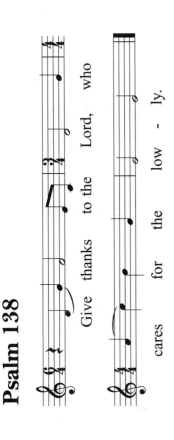

Give thanks to the Lord, who cares for the low-ly.

Psalm 138

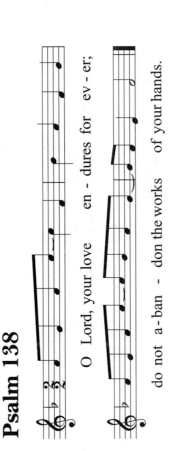

O Lord, your love en-dures for ev-er; do not a-ban-don the works of your hands.

Psalm 138

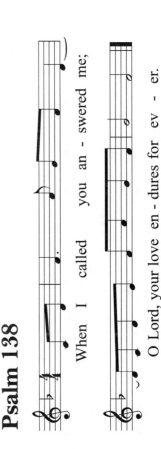

When I called you an-swered me; O Lord, your love en-dures for ev-er.

Congregational Refrains 147-Canticle 15

Psalm 147

How pleas - ant it is to ho - nor God with praise, hal - le - lu - jah.

Psalm 148

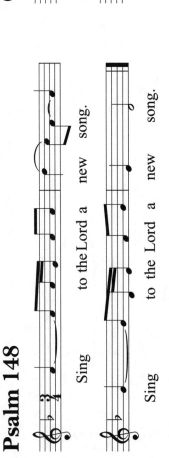

Sing to the Lord a new song. Sing to the Lord a new song.

Psalm 149

Sing to the Lord a new song. Sing to the Lord a new song.

Canticle 15

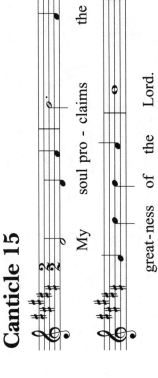

My soul pro - claims the great-ness of the Lord.